Scott Foresman
SCIENCE

Series Authors

Dr. Timothy Cooney
Professor of Earth Science and
*   Science Education*
Earth Science Department
University of Northern Iowa
Cedar Falls, Iowa

Michael Anthony DiSpezio
Science Education Specialist
Cape Cod Children's Museum
Falmouth, Massachusetts

Barbara K. Foots
Science Education Consultant
Houston, Texas

Dr. Angie L. Matamoros
Science Curriculum Specialist
Broward County Schools
Ft. Lauderdale, Florida

Kate Boehm Nyquist
Science Writer and Curriculum Specialist
Mount Pleasant, South Carolina

Dr. Karen L. Ostlund
Professor
Science Education Center
The University of Texas at Austin
Austin, Texas

Contributing Authors

Dr. Anna Uhl Chamot
Associate Professor and
*   ESL Faculty Advisor*
Department of Teacher Preparation
   and Special Education
Graduate School of Education
   and Human Development
The George Washington University
Washington, D.C.

Dr. Jim Cummins
Professor
Modern Language Centre and
   Curriculum Department
Ontario Institute for Studies in Education
Toronto, Canada

Gale Philips Kahn
Lecturer, Science and Math Education
Elementary Education Department
California State University, Fullerton
Fullerton, California

Vincent Sipkovich
Teacher
Irvine Unified School District
Irvine, California

Steve Weinberg
Science Consultant
Connecticut State
   Department of Education
Hartford, Connecticut

Scott Foresman

Editorial Offices: Glenview, Illinois • Parsippany, New Jersey • New York, New York
Sales Offices: Parsippany, New Jersey • Duluth, Georgia • Glenview, Illinois
Carrollton, Texas • Ontario, California
www.sfscience.com

Content Consultants

Dr. J. Scott Cairns
National Institutes of Health
Bethesda, Maryland

Jackie Cleveland
Elementary Resource Specialist
Mesa Public School District
Mesa, Arizona

Robert L. Kolenda
Science Lead Teacher, K-12
Neshaminy School District
Langhorne, Pennsylvania

David P. Lopath
Teacher
The Consolidated School District
of New Britain
New Britain, Connecticut

Sammantha Lane Magsino
Science Coordinator
Institute of Geophysics
University of Texas at Austin
Austin, Texas

Kathleen Middleton
Director, Health Education
ToucanEd
Soquel, California

Irwin Slesnick
Professor of Biology
Western Washington University
Bellingham, Washington

Dr. James C. Walters
Professor of Geology
University of Northern Iowa
Cedar Falls, Iowa

Multicultural Consultants

Dr. Shirley Gholston Key
Assistant Professor
University of Houston-Downtown
Houston, Texas

Damon L. Mitchell
Quality Auditor
Louisiana-Pacific Corporation
Conroe, Texas

Classroom Reviewers

Kathleen Avery
Teacher
Kellogg Science/Technology Magnet
Wichita, Kansas

Margaret S. Brown
Teacher
Cedar Grove Primary
Williamston, South Carolina

Deborah Browne
Teacher
Whitesville Elementary School
Moncks Corner, South Carolina

Wendy Capron
Teacher
Corlears School
New York, New York

Jiwon Choi
Teacher
Corlears School
New York, New York

John Cirrincione
Teacher
West Seneca Central Schools
West Seneca, New York

Jacqueline Colander
Teacher
Norfolk Public Schools
Norfolk, Virginia

Dr. Terry Contant
Teacher
Conroe Independent
School District
The Woodlands, Texas

Susan Crowley-Walsh
Teacher
Meadowbrook Elementary School
Gladstone, Missouri

Charlene K. Dindo
Teacher
Fairhope K-1 Center/Pelican's Nest
Science Lab
Fairhope, Alabama

Laurie Duffee
Teacher
Barnard Elementary
Tulsa, Oklahoma

Beth Anne Ebler
Teacher
Newark Public Schools
Newark, New Jersey

Karen P. Farrell
Teacher
Rondout Elementary School
District #72
Lake Forest, Illinois

Anna M. Gaiter
Teacher
Los Angeles Unified School District
Los Angeles Systemic Initiative
Los Angeles, California

Federica M. Gallegos
Teacher
Highland Park Elementary
Salt Lake School District
Salt Lake City, Utah

Janet E. Gray
Teacher
Anderson Elementary - Conroe ISD
Conroe, Texas

Karen Guinn
Teacher
Ehrhardt Elementary School - KISD
Spring, Texas

Denis John Hagerty
Teacher
Al Ittihad Private Schools
Dubai, United Arab Emirates

Judith Halpern
Teacher
Bannockburn School
Deerfield, Illinois

Debra D. Harper
Teacher
Community School District 9
Bronx, New York

Gretchen Harr
Teacher
Denver Public Schools - Doull School
Denver, Colorado

Bonnie L. Hawthorne
Teacher
Jim Darcy School
School District #1
Helena, Montana

Marselle Heywood-Julian
Teacher
Community School District 6
New York, New York

Scott Klene
Teacher
Bannockburn School 106
Bannockburn, Illinois

Thomas Kranz
Teacher
Livonia Primary School
Livonia, New York

Tom Leahy
Teacher
Coos Bay School District
Coos Bay, Oregon

Mary Littig
Teacher
Kellogg Science/Technology Magnet
Wichita, Kansas

Patricia Marin
Teacher
Corlears School
New York, New York

Susan Maki
Teacher
Cotton Creek CUSD 118
Island Lake, Illinois

Efraín M.
Teacher
East LA Mathematics S
Center LAUSD
Los Angeles, California

Becky Mojalid
Teacher
Manarat Jeddah Girls' School
Jeddah, Saudi Arabia

Susan Nations
Teacher
Sulphur Springs Elementary
Tampa, Florida

Brooke Palmer
Teacher
Whitesville Elementary
Moncks Corner, South Carolina

Jayne Pedersen
Teacher
Laura B. Sprague
School District 103
Lincolnshire, Illinois

Shirley Pfingston
Teacher
Orland School District 135
Orland Park, Illinois

Teresa Gayle Rountree
Teacher
Box Elder School District
Brigham City, Utah

Helen C. Smith
Teacher
Schultz Elementary
Klein Independent School District
Tomball, Texas

Denette Smith-Gibson
Teacher
Mitchell Intermediate, CISD
The Woodlands, Texas

Mary Jean Syrek
Teacher
Dr. Charles R. Drew Science
Magnet
Buffalo, New York

Rosemary Troxel
Teacher
Libertyville School District 70
Libertyville, Illinois

Susan D. Vani
Teacher
Laura B. Sprague School
School District 103
Lincolnshire, Illinois

Debra Worman
Teacher
Bryant Elementary
Tulsa, Oklahoma

Dr. Gayla Wright
Teacher
Edmond Public School
Edmond, Oklahoma

ISBN: 0-328-03440-1

Activity and Safety Consultants

Laura Adams
Teacher
Holley-Navarre Intermediate
Navarre, Florida

Dr. Charlie Ashman
Teacher
Carl Sandburg Middle School
Mundelein District #75
Mundelein, Illinois

Christopher Atlee
Teacher
Horace Mann Elementary
Wichita Public Schools
Wichita, Kansas

David Bachman
Consultant
Chicago, Illinois

Sherry Baldwin
Teacher
Shady Brook
Bedford ISD
Euless, Texas

Pam Bazis
Teacher
Richardson ISD
   Classical Magnet School
Richardson, Texas

Angela Boese
Teacher
McCollom Elementary
Wichita Public Schools USD #259
Wichita, Kansas

Jan Buckelew
Teacher
Taylor Ranch Elementary
Venice, Florida

Shonie Castaneda
Teacher
Carman Elementary, PSJA
Pharr, Texas

Donna Coffey
Teacher
Melrose Elementary - Pinellas
St. Petersburg, Florida

Diamantina Contreras
Teacher
J.T. Brackenridge Elementary
San Antonio ISD
San Antonio, Texas

Susanna Curtis
Teacher
Lake Bluff Middle School
Lake Bluff, Illinois

Karen Farrell
Teacher
Rondout Elementary School,
   Dist. #72
Lake Forest, Illinois

Paul Gannon
Teacher
El Paso ISD
El Paso, Texas

Nancy Garman
Teacher
Jefferson Elementary School
Charleston, Illinois

Susan Graves
Teacher
Beech Elementary
Wichita Public Schools USD #259
Wichita, Kansas

Jo Anna Harrison
Teacher
Cornelius Elementary
Houston ISD
Houston, Texas

Monica Hartman
Teacher
Richard Elementary
Detroit Public Schools
Detroit, Michigan

Kelly Howard
Teacher
Sarasota, Florida

Kelly Kimborough
Teacher
Richardson ISD
   Classical Magnet School
Richardson, Texas

Mary Leveron
Teacher
Velasco Elementary
Brazosport ISD
Freeport, Texas

Becky McClendon
Teacher
A.P. Beutel Elementary
Brazosport ISD
Freeport, Texas

Suzanne Milstead
Teacher
Liestman Elementary
Alief ISD
Houston, Texas

Debbie Oliver
Teacher
School Board of Broward County
Ft. Lauderdale, Florida

Sharon Pearthree
Teacher
School Board of Broward County
Ft. Lauderdale, Florida

Jayne Pedersen
Teacher
Laura B. Sprague School
District 103
Lincolnshire, Illinois

Sharon Pedroja
Teacher
Riverside Cultural
   Arts/History Magnet
Wichita Public Schools USD #259
Wichita, Kansas

Marcia Percell
Teacher
Pharr, San Juan, Alamo ISD
Pharr, Texas

Shirley Pfingston
Teacher
Orland School District #135
Orland Park, Illinois

Sharon S. Placko
Teacher
District 26, Mt. Prospect
Mt. Prospect, IL

Glenda Rall
Teacher
Seltzer Elementary
USD #259
Wichita, Kansas

Nelda Requenez
Teacher
Canterbury Elementary
Edinburg, Texas

Dr. Beth Rice
Teacher
Loxahatchee Groves
   Elementary School
Loxahatchee, Florida

Martha Salom Romero
Teacher
El Paso ISD
El Paso, Texas

Paula Sanders
Teacher
Welleby Elementary School
Sunrise, Florida

Lynn Setchell
Teacher
Sigsbee Elementary School
Key West, Florida

Rhonda Shook
Teacher
Mueller Elementary
Wichita Public Schools USD #259
Wichita, Kansas

Anna Marie Smith
Teacher
Orland School District #135
Orland Park, Illinois

Nancy Ann Varneke
Teacher
Seltzer Elementary
Wichita Public Schools USD #259
Wichita, Kansas

Aimee Walsh
Teacher
Rolling Meadows, Illinois

Ilene Wagner
Teacher
O.A. Thorp Scholastic Acacemy
Chicago Public Schools
Chicago, Illinois

Brian Warren
Teacher
Riley Community Consolidated
   School District 18
Marengo, Illinois

Tammie White
Teacher
Holley-Navarre
   Intermediate School
Navarre, Florida

Dr. Mychael Willon
Principal
Horace Mann Elementary
Wichita Public Schools
Wichita, Kansas

Inclusion Consultants

Dr. Eric J. Pyle, Ph.D.
Assistant Professor, Science Education
Department of Educational Theory
   and Practice
West Virginia University
Morgantown, West Virginia

Dr. Gretchen Butera, Ph.D.
Associate Professor, Special Education
Department of Education Theory
   and Practice
West Virginia University
Morgantown, West Virginia

Bilingual Consultant

Irma Gomez-Torres
Dalindo Elementary
Austin ISD
Austin, Texas

Bilingual Reviewers

Mary E. Morales
E.A. Jones Elementary
Fort Bend ISD
Missouri City, Texas

Gabriela T. Nolasco
Pebble Hills Elementary
Ysleta ISD
El Paso, Texas

Maribel B. Tanguma
Reed and Mock Elementary
San Juan, Texas

Yesenia Garza
Reed and Mock Elementary
San Juan, Texas

Teri Gallegos
St. Andrew's School
Austin, Texas

**Go to PHYSICAL SCIENCE
UNIT B Table of Contents**

Unit B
Physical Science

Here is the Table of Contents

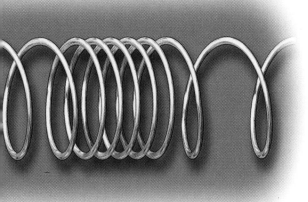

**Go to PHYSICAL SCIENCE
UNIT B Table of Contents**

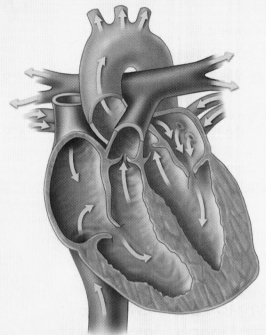

Unit D
Human Body

Your Science Handbook

Go to PHYSICAL SCIENCE UNIT B Table of Contents

Using Scientific Methods for Science Inquiry

Scientists try to solve many problems. Scientists study problems in different ways, but they all use scientific methods to guide their work. Scientific methods are organized ways of finding answers and solving problems. Scientific methods include the steps shown on these pages. The order of the steps or the number of steps used may change. You can use these steps to organize your own scientific inquiries.

State the Problem

The problem is the question you want to answer. Curiosity and inquiry have resulted in many scientific discoveries. State your problem in the form of a question.

Which clay boat design holds more marbles before sinking?

Formulate Your Hypothesis

Your hypothesis is a possible answer to your problem. Make sure your hypothesis can be tested. Your hypothesis should take the form of a statement.

◀ *A wide boat with high sides holds more marbles.*

Identify and Control the Variables

For a fair test, you must select which variable to change and which variables to control. Choose one variable to change when you test your hypothesis. Control the other variables so they do not change.

▲ *Make one boat wide and the other boat narrow. Both boats will have high sides. Use the same amount of clay for each boat.*

Test Your Hypothesis

Do experiments to test your hypothesis. You may need to repeat experiments to make sure your results remain consistent. Sometimes you conduct a scientific survey to test a hypothesis.

◀ Place marbles in the boat until it sinks. Repeat for the other boat.

Collect Your Data

As you test your hypothesis, you will collect data about the problem you want to solve. You may need to record measurements. You might make drawings or diagrams. Or you may write lists or descriptions. Collect as much data as you can while testing your hypothesis.

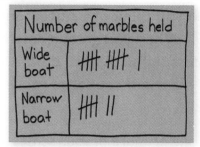

Number of marbles held

| Wide boat | HHT HHT I |
| Narrow boat | HHT II |

Interpret Your Data

By organizing your data into charts, tables, diagrams, and graphs, you may see patterns in the data. Then you can decide what the information from your data means.

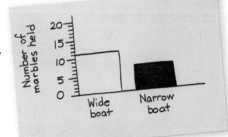

State Your Conclusion

Your conclusion is a decision you make based on evidence. Compare your results with your hypothesis. Based on whether or not your data supports your hypothesis, decide if your hypothesis is correct or incorrect. Then communicate your conclusion by stating or presenting your decision.

A wide boat design holds more marbles!

❓ Inquire Further

Use what you learn to solve other problems or to answer other questions that you might have. You may decide to repeat your experiment, or to change it based on what you learned.

▼ Will the results be similar with aluminum foil boats?

Using Process Skills for Science Inquiry

These 12 process skills are used by scientists when they do their research. You also use many of these skills every day. For example, when you think of a statement that you can test, you are using process skills. When you gather data to make a chart or graph, you are using process skills. As you do the activities in your book, you will use these same process skills.

I see..., I smell..., I hear..., It feels like..., I never taste without permission!

Observing
Use one or more of your senses—seeing, hearing, smelling, touching, or tasting—to gather information about objects or events.

Communicating
Share information about what you learn using words, pictures, charts, graphs, and diagrams.

Classifying
Arrange or group objects according to their common properties.

◀ Rocks with one color in Group 1.

Rocks with two or more colors in Group 2. ▶

Estimating and Measuring
Make an estimate about an object's properties, then measure and describe the object in units.

It's as heavy as a... It sounds like a... It must be shaped like a...

Inferring
Draw a conclusion or make a reasonable guess based on what you observe, or from your past experiences.

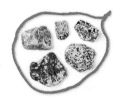

Predicting

Form an idea about what will happen based on evidence.

◀ *Predict what happens after 15 minutes.*

An electromagnet is a coil of wire around a bolt that... ▶

Making Operational Definitions

Define or describe an object or event based on your experiences with it.

Making and Using Models

Make real or mental representations to explain ideas, objects, or events.

◀ *It's different from a real bridge because...*
The model is like a real bridge because...

If you place a plant by a sunny window, the leaves will... ▶

Formulating Questions and Hypotheses

Think of a statement that you can test to solve a problem or to answer a question about how something works.

Collecting and Interpreting Data

Gather observations and measurements into graphs, tables, charts, or diagrams. Then use the information to solve problems or answer questions.

The plant in the polluted water grew the slowest.

Identifying and Controlling Variables

Change one factor that may affect the outcome of an event while holding other factors constant.

Variables

Change	Same
✓ Amount of fertilizer	✓ Temperature
	✓ Plant size
	✓ Water
	✓ Light
	✓ Soil

Experimenting

Design an investigation to test a hypothesis or to solve a problem. Then form a conclusion.

I'll write a clear procedure so that other students could repeat the experiment.

? Science Inquiry

Throughout your science book, you will ask questions, do investigations, answer your questions, and tell others what you have learned. Use the descriptions below to help you during your scientific inquiry.

What kind of cup keeps liquid colder?

1 Ask a question about objects, organisms, and events in the environment.

You will find the answer to your question from your own observations and investigations and from reliable sources of scientific information.

2 Plan and conduct a simple investigation.

The kind of investigation you do depends on the question you ask. Kinds of investigations include describing objects, events, and organisms; classifying them; and doing a fair test or experiment.

3 Use simple equipment and tools to gather data and extend the senses.

Equipment and tools you might use include rulers and meter sticks, compasses, thermometers, watches, balances, spring scales, hand lenses, microscopes, cameras, calculators, and computers.

4 Use data to construct a reasonable explanation.

Use the information that you have gathered to answer your question and support your answer. Compare your answer to scientific knowledge, your experiences, and the observations of others.

5 Communicate investigations and explanations.

Share your work with others by writing, drawing, or talking. Describe your work in a way that others could repeat your investigation.

Question
what kind of cup
keeps liquid colder?
materials
thermometer
paper cup
clear plastic cup
plastic foam cup
water

Unit B
Physical Science

Science and Technology
In Your World!

Tiny Chips Power Amazing Games!

Did you know that dozens of computer chips can fit on the head of a pin? Video games use these chips to power games so real you think you are there! Years of studying matter came before the invention of computer chips. You will learn about matter in **Chapter 1 Measuring Matter.**

Get in Gear!

In the late 1800s, bicycle pedals were attached directly to the front wheel. Tires were steel or solid rubber! Inventors and engineers use their knowledge of forces, work, and machines to make bicycles better and better. You will learn about forces, work, and machines in **Chapter 2 Force and Motion.**

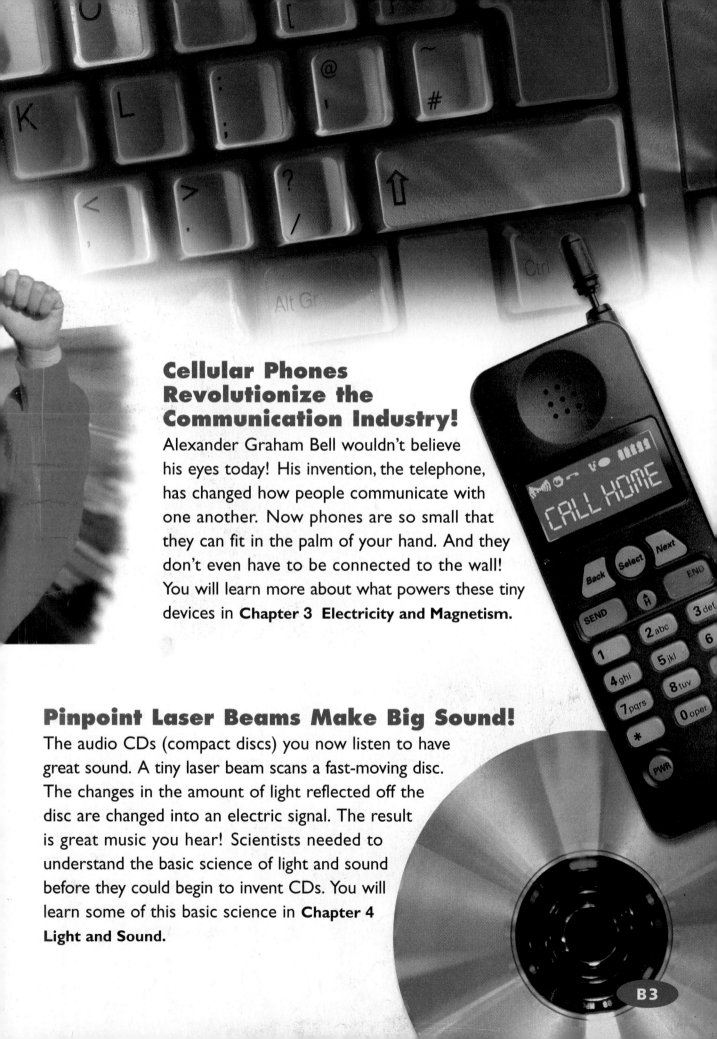

Cellular Phones Revolutionize the Communication Industry!

Alexander Graham Bell wouldn't believe his eyes today! His invention, the telephone, has changed how people communicate with one another. Now phones are so small that they can fit in the palm of your hand. And they don't even have to be connected to the wall! You will learn more about what powers these tiny devices in **Chapter 3 Electricity and Magnetism.**

Pinpoint Laser Beams Make Big Sound!

The audio CDs (compact discs) you now listen to have great sound. A tiny laser beam scans a fast-moving disc. The changes in the amount of light reflected off the disc are changed into an electric signal. The result is great music you hear! Scientists needed to understand the basic science of light and sound before they could begin to invent CDs. You will learn some of this basic science in **Chapter 4 Light and Sound.**

What's the Matter?

Everything around you is made of matter that can be measured. How much matter do you think there is in an apple?

Chapter 1
Measuring Matter

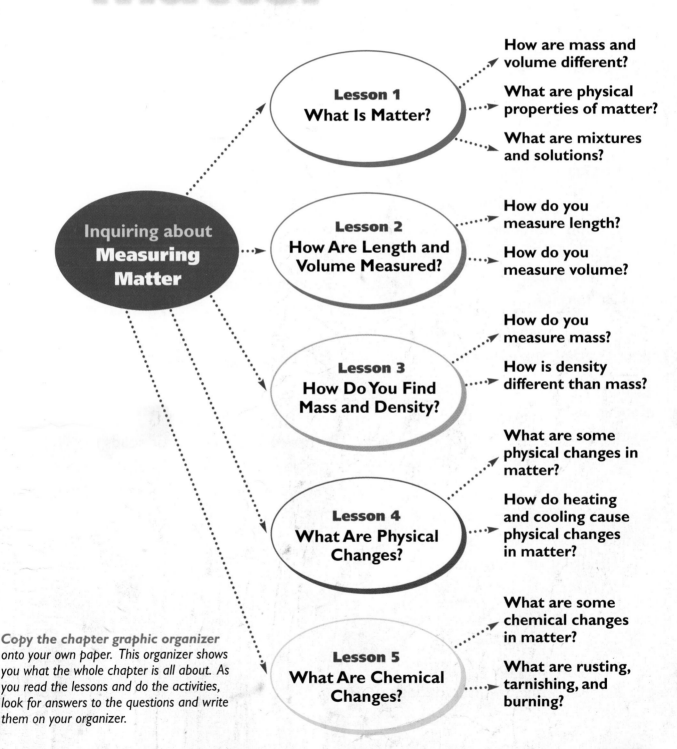

Inquiring about Measuring Matter

Lesson 1
What Is Matter?

How are mass and volume different?

What are physical properties of matter?

What are mixtures and solutions?

Lesson 2
How Are Length and Volume Measured?

How do you measure length?

How do you measure volume?

Lesson 3
How Do You Find Mass and Density?

How do you measure mass?

How is density different than mass?

Lesson 4
What Are Physical Changes?

What are some physical changes in matter?

How do heating and cooling cause physical changes in matter?

Lesson 5
What Are Chemical Changes?

What are some chemical changes in matter?

What are rusting, tarnishing, and burning?

Copy the chapter graphic organizer onto your own paper. This organizer shows you what the whole chapter is all about. As you read the lessons and do the activities, look for answers to the questions and write them on your organizer.

Exploring Matter

Process Skills

- observing
- communicating
- inferring

Materials

- water in plastic cup
- syrup in plastic cup
- vegetable oil in plastic cup
- celery
- modeling clay
- raisin
- aluminum foil

Explore

1 In this activity you will explore some properties of liquids and solids. Make a list of the materials. Leave room by each item to record observations.

2 Observe each item and write three words to describe each one.

3 Slowly pour the water into the cup of syrup as shown. Then pour the vegetable oil into the cup. Record your observations of the syrup, water, and vegetable oil.

4 Carefully drop the celery, the modeling clay, and the raisin into the cup. Record your observations for each item.

5 Tear the aluminum foil into two pieces. Squeeze one piece into a tight ball. Put both foil pieces in the cup. Record your observations.

Reflect

1. Communicate. Compare and contrast your observations with those of other groups.

2. Think about the layers of liquids. Make an **inference.** Which do you think has greater mass, 30 mL of syrup or 30 mL of vegetable oil? Explain.

? Inquire Further

What common liquids or solids might float in vegetable oil? Develop a plan to answer this or other questions you may have.

Exploring Mass

Kim Brownfield's wheelchair doesn't keep him from setting world records. His record lift of 237 kilograms earned him a gold medal at the Paralympic Games in 1996. A **kilogram** is a metric unit of mass. Below you will learn about another metric unit of mass, the **gram**.

Working Together

Use a **balance**, gram cubes, a nickel, and small classroom objects to explore mass.

1. Use the balance and gram cubes to find the mass of the nickel.

2. Choose a small object, such as a piece of chalk. Hold it in one hand. Hold the nickel in the other hand. Do you think the mass of the object is greater or less than the mass of the nickel? Use the balance to check.

3. Is the mass of a penny greater or less than 5 grams? How could you find out without using the balance?

4. Choose 5 small objects. Estimate which have a mass greater than 5 grams and which have a mass less than 5 grams. Use the nickel and the balance scale to check.

Talk About It!

1. Which is greater, a gram or a kilogram?

2. A cotton ball and a marble are about the same size. The mass of the cotton ball is less than 1 gram, but the mass of the marble is about 10 grams. How can you explain their difference in mass?

Materials
- balance
- gram cubes
- a penny
- a nickel
- small classroom objects

Math Vocabulary

balance, an instrument used to measure an object's mass

gram (g), a metric unit of mass

kilogram (kg), a metric unit of mass equal to 1,000 grams

You will learn:

- how mass and volume are different.
- what physical properties of matter are.
- what mixtures and solutions are.

Glossary

matter (mat′ər), anything that has mass and takes up space

mass (mas), the amount of material that an object has in it

volume (vol′yəm), the amount of space that matter takes up

Lesson 1

What Is Matter?

Big, twisted pretzels and small, twisted pretzels. Long, thick pretzels and short, skinny pretzels. These pretzels all have one thing in common. They are all made of matter—the same kind of matter!

Mass and Volume

Just like the pretzels, you, a car, and a dog all are made of matter. In fact, all living and nonliving things, even your socks, are made of matter. **Matter** is anything that has mass and takes up space. **Mass** is the amount of material that an object has in it.

The two pretzels shown below are made up of matter. Both of the pretzels have mass and take up space. However, one of the pretzels is thicker than the other. The pretzels are made of the same material. The thinner pretzel has less mass because it is made of less material.

The thinner pretzel also takes up less space. It has less volume than the thicker pretzel. **Volume** is the amount of space that matter takes up.

Both of these pretzels have volume. Which pretzel has more volume? ▶

Physical Properties of Matter

Think about the last time you described a new toy to a friend. You probably described it by its color, shape, and size. You described the properties of the toy. A property is something about matter that can be observed and tells you what the matter is like. Color, shape, size, and mass are some physical properties of matter. These properties can be used to describe or sort matter.

One important property of matter is the state, or form, that matter has. Matter has three states—solid, liquid, and gas. A solid has a shape and a volume of its own. Your desk and books are solids.

A liquid has a certain volume, but it has no shape of its own. A liquid takes the shape of its container. Milk and water are liquids. The boy below is pouring soapy water into a bowl. What shape do you think the water will take?

The air you breathe is made up of gases. Notice the girl blowing air into the soapy water to make bubbles. The air in the soap bubbles takes the shape of the bubbles. A gas, like a liquid, does not have a shape of its own. Unlike a liquid, a gas does not have a volume of its own. When the bubbles break, the gases spread out and take up more space.

States of matter include solid, liquid, and gas. Find a solid, a liquid, and a gas in the picture. ▼

Some materials have the ability to float and others do not. ▶

Another property of matter is the ability of some matter to float in a gas or liquid. An onion and a piece of celery are floating in the water in one of the bowls in the picture. The potato and carrot in the other bowl are not floating. They sank to the bottom of the water.

Mixtures and Solutions

You can mix matter together in different ways. For example, you can cut up lettuce, cucumbers, and carrots and mix them with tomatoes to make a vegetable salad. Notice the vegetable salad in the picture. You can see that the pieces of vegetables have the same colors and other properties that they had before being mixed together. The pieces of vegetables can also be easily separated. They have not joined together to make a new substance.

A salad is one kind of mixture. ▼

The vegetable salad is one kind of mixture. A **mixture** is two or more substances that are mixed together but can easily be separated. Mixtures can have different kinds and amounts of substances. The salad could have different amounts of each vegetable or different kinds of vegetables.

Another kind of mixture forms when you mix salt and water together. The salt dissolves in the water. Notice the glass of salt water in the picture. You cannot see the salt. When it dissolves, the salt breaks into tiny bits that are too small to see. These bits spread out evenly through the water. The water and salt become a kind of mixture called a solution. A **solution** is a mixture in which one substance spreads evenly throughout another substance. However, the salt and water can be separated. Let the glass sit in a warm place until the water evaporates. The salt will be left in the glass.

Glossary

mixture (miks′chər), two or more substances that are mixed together but can be easily separated

solution (sə lü′shən), a mixture in which one substance spreads evenly throughout another substance

▲ *Now you see it, now you don't! Salt disappears as it dissolves in water.*

Lesson 1 Review

1. How are the mass and volume of an object different?

2. What are two physical properties of matter?

3. How is a solution different from other mixtures?

4. **Mass**
   Which would you estimate has the greater mass—a 6 cm piece of celery or a 6 cm carrot? How can you check your estimate?

You will learn:

- how to measure length.
- how to measure volume.

Lesson 2

How Are Length and Volume Measured?

How tall are you? How long is your arm? What length is your foot? What volume of matter can you hold in your hands? To find the answers, you need to measure length and volume!

Measuring Length

A meter stick is a measuring tool that can be used to accurately measure length. ▼

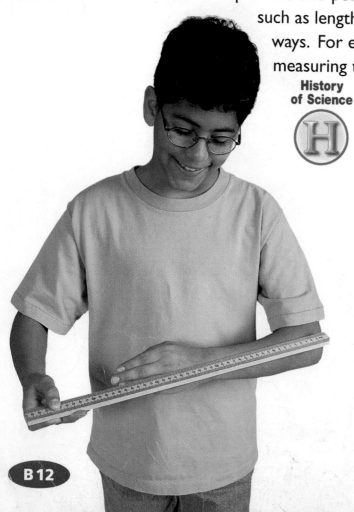

Length is a property of matter. Length measures the distance between one point and another, or how far apart the two points are. People use measurements, such as length, to help describe matter in exact ways. For example, the boy in the picture is measuring the length of his lower arm and hand.

History of Science H

In ancient times, people used their body parts or things in nature to measure. Fingers, hands, and arms were measuring tools. For example, people measured a horse by how many hands high it was.

Scientists found that using body parts to measure was not very accurate. When different people measured the same object, their measurements were not always the same. Can you think of reasons why using body parts such as your arms to measure might not be accurate?

Prefixes for Meter

centi- means $\frac{1}{100}$	centimeter (cm) = $\frac{1}{100}$ of a meter
milli- means $\frac{1}{1,000}$	millimeter (mm) = $\frac{1}{1,000}$ of a meter
kilo- means 1,000	kilometer (km) = 1,000 meters

In 1790, France passed a law making the metric system of measurement its standard. Today, this system is used in most countries. In the metric system, a unit for measuring length is the **meter.** The symbol for meter is m. To measure the width of a desk, you would use a meter stick as the boy in the picture is. A meter stick is divided into 100 equal parts called centimeters. Find the centimeter marks on the meter stick to the right. The symbol for centimeter is cm. The prefix *centi-* means $\frac{1}{100}$.

A meter stick is also divided into 1,000 tiny, equal parts called millimeters. The prefix *milli-* means $\frac{1}{1,000}$. The symbol for millimeter is mm. Find the millimeter marks on the meter stick shown.

A kilometer is 1,000 meters. The prefix *kilo-* means 1,000. The symbol for kilometer is km. Kilometers are used to measure long distances, such as the distance between two cities or how tall a mountain is.

How long is this paper clip in millimeters? in centimeters? ▼

This boy is using a meter stick to measure the width of a desk. ▶

Measuring Volume

Like length, volume is a property of matter that can be measured. Suppose you want to know how much a box will hold. Like people in ancient times, you might use things around you to measure volume. You might fill the box with smaller boxes. But if other people measure using different-sized boxes, they might get a different volume than you do.

To measure something accurately, it's best to use the same tools scientists use. One way to measure the volume of a solid is by using a meter stick, as the children in the picture are doing. To find out the volume of a box, first measure the length, width, and height of the box. Then multiply the length times the width times the height. If the box measures 2 meters long, 2 meters wide, and 1 meter high, multiply 2 meters × 2 meters × 1 meter. The volume of the box is 4 cubic meters. A **cubic meter** is a unit for measuring volume. A cube 1 meter long, 1 meter wide, and 1 meter high is a cubic meter. If the box is 4 cubic meters, it means that the box can hold four cubes that are 1 meter × 1 meter × 1 meter.

Volume also is often measured in liters. Liquids like juices are sold in liters. A **liter** is another unit for measuring volume. The symbol for liter is L. A milliliter is equal to $\frac{1}{1,000}$ of a liter. The symbol for milliliter is mL. Medicines are sometimes measured in milliliters.

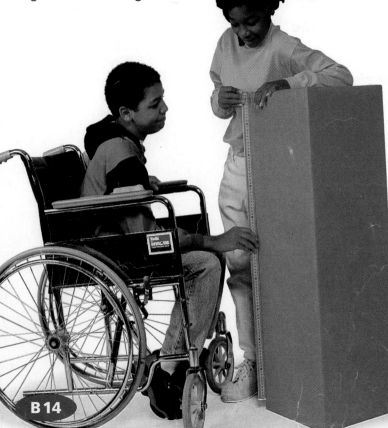

To measure the volume of a box, first measure its length, width, and height. Then multiply length X width X height. ▼

Scientists use a special kind of measuring tool called a graduated cylinder to measure the volume of liquids. A **graduated cylinder** is marked with lines that are equal distances apart.

A graduated cylinder can be used to measure the volume of an object that has an irregular length, width, or height. To measure the volume of a hard solid, like a small rock, fill a graduated cylinder with water. Record the height of the water in the graduated cylinder. Place the rock inside the graduated cylinder and record the height of the water. Subtract the first measurement from the second measurement. The difference is the volume of the rock, or the space the rock takes up. What is the volume of the rock in the picture?

Glossary

graduated cylinder
(graj′ü ā′tid sil′ən dər), a tool used to measure the volume of liquids

Glossary

When the rock is dropped into the water, it takes up space. The space the rock takes up is its volume. ▶

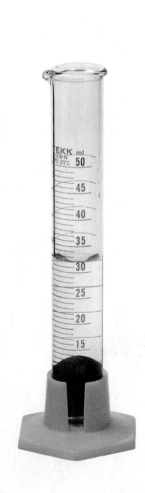

Lesson 2 Review

1. What unit would you use to measure the length of your classroom?

2. What are two different units scientists use to measure volume?

3. **Mass**
   Which would you estimate has the greater mass—a rock with a volume of 1 mL or a rock with a volume of 4 mL? How can you check your estimate?

You will learn:

- how to measure the mass of an object.
- what the difference between mass and density is.

Lesson 3

How Do You Find Mass and Density?

Here's a riddle for you: Which has more mass—a kilogram of gold or a kilogram of feathers? **Right!** They both have the same mass.

Measuring Mass

Like length and volume, mass is a property of matter that can be measured. Mass is closely related to how heavy something is, but weight and mass are not the same thing.

Sometimes you can tell that one object has more mass than another. It just feels heavier. The child in the picture is trying to compare the mass of two objects by lifting them. However, for things that are about the same mass, a balance like the one on the next page can help you find out which object has the most mass.

◄ *The box of chalk and the box of crayons are the same size, but they have different masses.*

Some metric units used to measure mass are gram, milligram, and kilogram. The **gram** is the basic unit for measuring mass. A small paper clip has about 1 gram of mass. A milligram is $\frac{1}{1,000}$ of a gram. Substances that are used in small amounts, such as vitamins and medicines, are usually measured in milligrams. A kilogram is equal to 1,000 grams. Kilograms are useful in measuring the mass of large objects. The mass of a person is measured in kilograms.

The girl in the picture below is balancing a box of crayons with objects of a known mass. First the girl placed the crayons on the balance. The pan with the crayons in it moved down. Now the girl is placing the known objects on the balance. When the two pans on the balance are even, she will stop adding objects. By adding together the masses of the known objects, the girl knows the mass of the crayons.

Now look at the balance on the right. A box of crayons is on one side and a box of chalk is on the other side of the balance. Which has more mass—the crayons or the chalk? How do you know?

A balance can help you find the mass of an object, or which of two objects has the most mass. ▼

The red vinegar and oil have the same volume but a different density. ▼

Density

Density is another property of matter. Have you ever helped an adult mix vinegar and oil to make salad dressing? Watching what happens to the vinegar and oil in the salad dressing can help you find out about density. The salad dressing is a great example of the density of different liquids.

The girl in the picture below is mixing vinegar and oil to make salad dressing. The particles in the vinegar are mixed with the particles in the oil. The bottle contains the same volume of vinegar and oil—100 mL of red vinegar, 100 mL of oil, and some seasonings. Then the girl sets the bottle down for a few minutes.

The two liquids do not have the same mass. After sitting still in the bottle, what happened to the mixture? Yes! It separated! Why do you think the vinegar is on the bottom? The vinegar is denser. It has more matter in it than the same volume of oil does.

Density is how much mass is in a certain volume of matter. The 100 mL of vinegar has a greater mass than the 100 mL of oil does. Therefore, the vinegar sinks to the bottom of the bottle. The oil floats on top of the vinegar. The density of the vinegar is greater than the density of the oil.

Look at the balance. The cork and the wood each have a mass of about 1 gram. That is why they balance. However, notice the size of the piece of cork on the right and the size of the piece of wood on the left. It is easy to see that the volume of the cork is larger than the volume of the wood. Which object do you think is denser? The wood is denser because the small piece of wood has the same mass as the larger piece of cork. If the pieces of wood and cork were the same size, the mass of the cork would be less than the mass of the wood. Therefore, the wood has the greater density.

Now think about the riddle at the beginning of the lesson. A kilogram of gold has the same mass as a kilogram of feathers, but which has the greater density? Think about how light a feather is. Imagine how many feathers it would take to have a kilogram of mass. So which has the greater density—gold or feathers?

▲ The wood and the cork have the same mass, but they have different volumes.

Lesson 3 Review

1. What metric units are used to measure mass?

2. How is density different than mass?

3. **Mass**
   Is the mass of a cup of water greater or less than the mass of a cup of rocks? How can you check your answer?

Describing and Measuring Matter

Process Skills

- observing
- estimating and measuring
- classifying

Materials

- rubber stopper
- 2 plastic cups
- balance
- masking tape
- gram cubes
- water
- graduated cylinder
- measuring cup
- paper towels
- steel bearing
- cork
- pencil

Getting Ready

In this activity you will practice describing and measuring properties of matter.

Follow This Procedure

1 Make a chart like the one shown. Use your chart to record your observations and measurements.

	Properties of matter		
Object			
Description			
Mass			
Volume of water in cylinder			
Volume after adding object			
Volume of object (mL)			

2 Place one plastic cup at each end of the balance. Use masking tape to attach each cup to the balance. Be sure the two cups are in balance.

3 **Observe** and describe the shape, color or colors, hardness, and any other properties of the rubber stopper. Record your observations.

Photo A

Photo B

4 **Measure** the mass of the rubber stopper. Place the rubber stopper in one of the cups. Observe what happens. Add gram cubes to the other cup until both cups are balanced (Photo A). Record your measurements in the chart.

5 Measure the volume of the rubber stopper. Pour water into a graduated cylinder until it is about half full. Record the volume of water in the cylinder.

6 Put the rubber stopper in the water. Record the new water level (Photo B).

7 Subtract the first water level from the second to find the volume of the rubber stopper. Record the volume. Carefully pour the rubber stopper and water into the measuring cup and remove the rubber stopper. Dry it with a paper towel and set it aside.

8 Repeat steps 2–7 using the steel bearing.

9 Repeat steps 2–7 using the cork. When you put the cork in water, use a pencil to hold it just under the surface of the water.

Interpret Your Results

Classify the objects by mass and volume. Rank the objects from least mass to greatest mass. Then rank the objects from least volume to greatest volume. Does the object with the greatest mass have the greatest volume?

 Inquire Further

How can you find the volume of an object bigger than the graduated cylinder? Develop a plan to answer this or other questions you may have.

Self-Assessment

- I followed instructions to describe and measure properties of matter.
- I **observed** and described shape, color, hardness, and other properties of three objects.
- I **measured** the mass and volume of each object.
- I recorded my observations and measurements.
- I **classified** the objects and ranked them by mass and volume.

Lesson 4

What Are Physical Changes?

DRIP! Water melts from an ice cube. **SNIP!** Scissors cut paper into bits. **SPLAT!** Clay smashes flat or crumbles into bits. **BOING!** A rubber band breaks. In these and other ways, physical changes can happen to matter.

Glossary

physical (fiz′ə kəl) **change,** a change in matter that changes physical properties, but does not produce a different kind of matter

Physical Changes in Matter

Matter goes through changes. Sometimes the changes are rather slow, as when a puddle of water dries up. Sometimes the changes are rather fast, as when a glass slips from your hand and you see it break.

Changes in the shape, size, color, or state of matter are some examples of physical changes. A **physical change** does not change matter into a different kind of matter. For example, the paper the child in the picture is painting is being changed. However, the paper is still paper. It is just a different color. Also, the cut paper, the clay, and the play dough can change shape, but they are still the same kind of matter. Only the physical properties of the matter are changed.

Heating and Cooling Matter

Another way to change matter is by heating or cooling it. Heating or cooling matter to certain temperatures causes matter to change state. A solid can become a liquid, and a liquid can become a solid or a gas.

When the temperature of a solid rises enough, it melts. Steel, rock, glass, plastic, butter, and ice—all these things melt when they reach a certain temperature. Steel, rock, and glass must reach very high temperatures before they start to melt. On the other hand, plastic, butter, and ice melt at lower temperatures.

Look at the picture of the ice. Notice the temperature on the thermometer. A temperature of 0°C isn't very high, but it is high enough for ice to melt. As the temperature of the ice rises, the ice changes state. It changes from a solid to a liquid. The **melting point** of a material is the temperature at which it melts and becomes a liquid.

Notice that the temperature of the water is 100°C. This is the boiling point of water. The **boiling point** of a material is the temperature at which it boils. It is also the temperature at which a material changes from a liquid to a gas. The bubbles you see rising in boiling water are gases. The gas bubbles form in water as it begins to boil. The gas escapes into the air.

The melting point and the boiling point of water are some of its physical properties. ▼

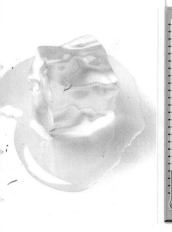

Glossary

freezing (frē′zing) **point,** the temperature at which matter changes from a liquid to a solid

Energy must be added to matter for the matter to melt or boil. Adding energy causes the temperature of the matter to rise. When the temperature of the matter reaches the melting point or the boiling point, the matter changes state.

Matter is cooled when energy is lost. When the temperature of water drops to 0°C, the water changes from a liquid to a solid—ice. This is called the freezing point of water.

The **freezing point** of a substance is the temperature at which the substance changes from a liquid to a solid. However, the freezing point of many substances is not very cold. For example, many substances, such as butter, are solids at room temperature. Their freezing point is much higher than 0°C.

The pictures on the next page show how heating and cooling are used to make crayons. When crayons are made, energy is added to solid wax. As the bits of matter that make up the wax gain energy, they move faster. As the particles move farther apart, the wax becomes a liquid. The liquid wax can be stirred and mixed with other materials. Dyes are added to the wax to give the crayons their colors.

The melted wax is placed in forms that give the crayons their shape. The cold water causes the wax to lose energy and cool. When the wax reaches its freezing point, it becomes a solid.

1 First, paraffin wax or beeswax gets heated until it melts.

2 The melted wax is mixed with pigments, or colored materials.

3 The hot, liquid crayon material is poured into crayon-shaped holes in a large mold. Cold water chills the mold until the crayons harden.

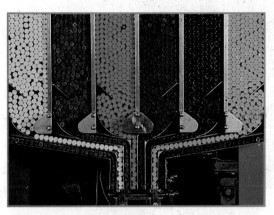

4 Each cooled, solid crayon is wrapped in a label. Finished crayons are placed into boxes and sent to stores.

Now you can use the crayons! ▼

Lesson 4 Review

1. Name four physical changes that can happen to material.

2. How does heating and cooling cause changes in matter?

3. Main Idea
What is the main idea of the last paragraph on page B24?

You will learn:

- about chemical changes in matter.
- how rusting, tarnishing, and burning are chemical changes.

What Are Chemical Changes?

WHIRRR! **SIZZLE!** You mix pancake batter and pour some on a hot griddle. The batter puffs up as bubbles form inside it. You flip the pancakes over. Chemical changes have changed the batter into pancakes.

Glossary

chemical change (kem′ə kəl chānj), a change in matter that produces a different kind of matter

Chemical Changes in Matter

Unlike a physical change, a **chemical change** produces a completely different kind of matter. In a chemical change, the matter produced by the change may have very different properties from the original matter.

Chemical Changes in Pancakes
Pancake batter is a liquid mixture of eggs, oil, milk, baking powder, salt, and flour. ▶

The pictures on these two pages show an example of a chemical change—making pancakes. To make pancakes, you mix some ingredients together as a liquid batter. As the batter cooks, a change takes place. The batter on the griddle browns and hardens as it cooks.

As the liquid batter on the griddle changes, another change also takes place. A gas is formed by the ingredients in the batter. The gas bubbles form inside the batter, rise to the top, and escape into the air. The rising bubbles fluff up the pancake and leave tiny air pockets. The liquid batter changes into a browned, spongy, solid pancake.

▲ *During cooking, bubbles of gas form and rise to the top of the batter. The batter browns and hardens into a spongy, solid, cakelike material.*

Human Body

When you eat the pancakes or any food, many chemical changes take place. Chemical changes even take place in your mouth.

As you chew, your saliva starts to break down the food into different substances. Inside your body, food goes through more chemical changes. Your body uses some of the substances produced for energy. Some of these materials are used to grow and repair your body parts.

◄ *When you eat pancakes, more chemical changes take place as your body digests the food.*

B27

Rusting, Tarnishing, and Burning

Some other examples of chemical changes are rusting, tarnishing, and burning. Each of these chemical changes produces different matter. Find out what matter is produced in the examples on these pages.

Rusting

◀ *Rust forms slowly as oxygen from the air joins with iron on the surface of a bicycle or other object that contains iron. Iron is hard and dark gray or black. Rust is orange-red and powdery or flaky. Rust has different properties from both air and iron. It is a different material formed by a chemical change.*

Tarnishing

Have you ever wondered why some coins look shiny and others look dull? Tarnish, like rust, forms slowly when air mixes with certain metals. On copper, tarnish looks dark brown or green. On silver, tarnish is black. On any metal, tarnish causes the metal to lose its shiny look. ▶

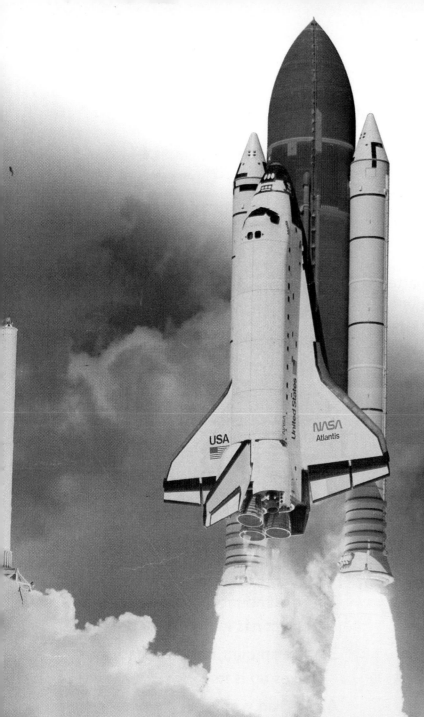

Burning

◀ *Exploding is the fastest kind of burning. The rocket boosters that lift the space shuttle into orbit contain liquid oxygen and liquid hydrogen fuel. When the oxygen and the hydrogen combine, they explode instantly and powerfully. The explosion releases energy whose force lifts the rocket from the surface of the earth. As the oxygen and hydrogen combine to form water, steam is given off.*

Lesson 5 Review

1. How does baking pancakes produce a different kind of matter?

2. Name three examples of chemical changes other than cooking.

3. Main Idea
What is the main idea of the paragraph on the bottom of page B28?

Chapter 1 Review

Chapter Main Ideas

Lesson 1
• Mass is the amount of material in matter, and volume is the amount of space that matter takes up.
• A property is something about matter that can be observed and tells you what the matter is like.
• Matter can be mixed together in solutions and other mixtures.

Lesson 2
• Length is measured in meters.
• Volume is measured in cubic meters or liters.

Lesson 3
• The metric system uses gram, milligram, and kilogram to measure mass.
• Density is how much mass is in a certain volume of matter.

Lesson 4
• A physical change is a change in size, shape, color, or state of matter.
• Heating and cooling cause physical changes in matter.

Lesson 5
• A chemical change produces a completely different kind of matter.
• Rusting, tarnishing, and burning are chemical changes of matter.

Reviewing Science Words and Concepts

Write the letter of the word or phrase that best completes each sentence.

a. boiling point
b. chemical change
c. cubic meter
d. density
e. freezing point
f. graduated cylinder
g. gram
h. liter
i. mass
j. matter
k. melting point
l. meter
m. mixture
n. physical change
o. solution
p. volume

1. Anything that has mass and takes up space is ___.
2. The amount of material that an object has in it is its ___.
3. The amount of space that a box takes up is its ___.
4. A salad is an example of a ___ because the vegetables can be easily separated.
5. A ___ is a kind of mixture in which a substance spreads evenly throughout another substance.
6. The unit you would use to measure the length of your classroom is a ___.

7. The unit for measuring the volume of a large box is a ___.

8. The unit used to measure the volume of a liquid is a ___.

9. To measure the volume of a liquid, scientists use a tool called a ___.

10. A ___ is the basic unit for measuring mass.

11. The amount of mass in a certain volume of matter is called ___.

12. A ___ does not produce a different kind of matter.

13. Water changes from ice to liquid water at its ___.

14. The temperature at which a liquid changes to a gas is its ___.

15. The ___ of water, or the temperature at which it changes from a liquid to a solid, is 0°C.

16. A change in matter, as in baking a cake, is an example of a ___.

Explaining Science

Draw and label a diagram or write a paragraph to explain each of the following.

1. What are physical properties of matter? Give three examples.

2. How would you measure the volume of a small piece of iron that has an irregular shape?

3. What are three metric units used to measure mass, and how is each unit used?

4. Ice cream melts at room temperature, but butter is a solid at room temperature. Explain how this is true.

5. How is a chemical change different from a physical change?

Using Skills

1. **Estimate** which has more **mass**— an apple or a lemon. How can you check your estimate?

2. A balloon filled with helium gas rises in the air. What might you **infer** about the density of helium as compared to the density of air?

3. Suppose you mix a substance in water and stir it well. Then you **observe** that tiny bits of the substance are floating in the water. From your observation, do you think this mixture is a solution? Why or why not?

Critical Thinking

1. Write a paragraph to **communicate** how heating and cooling causes matter to change from one state to another.

2. You fill a sink about three-fourths full of water. You turn a clear, plastic cup upside-down and push it into the water. The cup does not fill up with water, and it is hard to push into the water. **Draw a conclusion** about why the cup does not fill up with water.

Put Your Energy into Motion!

On your bike you slowly climb a hill. You use energy to pedal as hard as you can. You reach the top and apply the brakes to stop! Hey, that's friction!

Chapter 2
Force and Motion

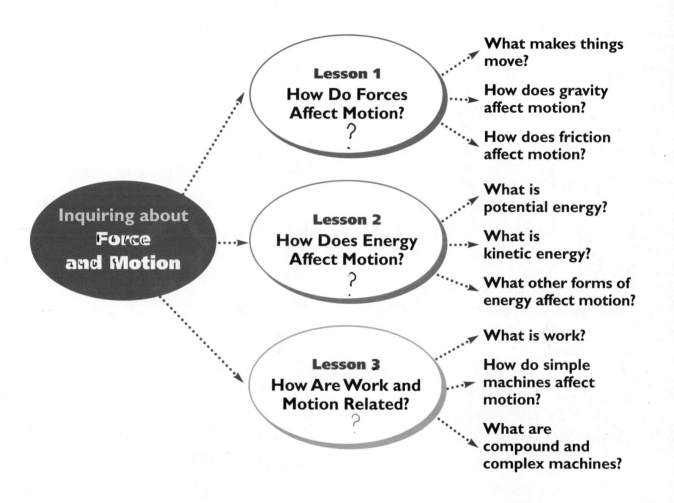

Inquiring about Force and Motion

Lesson 1
How Do Forces Affect Motion?
?

What makes things move?

How does gravity affect motion?

How does friction affect motion?

Lesson 2
How Does Energy Affect Motion?
?

What is potential energy?

What is kinetic energy?

What other forms of energy affect motion?

Lesson 3
How Are Work and Motion Related?
?

What is work?

How do simple machines affect motion?

What are compound and complex machines?

Copy the chapter graphic organizer onto your own paper. This organizer shows you what the whole chapter is all about. As you read the lessons and do the activities, look for answers to the questions and write them on your organizer.

Exploring Changes in Motion

Process Skills

- observing
- inferring

Materials

- safety goggles
- plastic cup
- index card
- quarter
- ball

Explore

1 Put on your safety goggles. Set the plastic cup on a flat surface and put an index card on top of the cup. Place a quarter in the center of the card.

2 Hold on to the cup. With your other hand, use your thumb and index finger to flick the card off the cup as shown. **Observe** and record what happens to the card and the coin.

3 Place the ball in the plastic cup, then put the cup on its side on the floor. Hold on to the cup as you rapidly slide it, open end forward, across the floor. Stop the cup suddenly and observe what happens to the ball. Record your observations.

Reflect

1. What caused the card to move sideways? What caused the quarter to move down?

2. Why did the ball continue to move when you stopped the cup? What finally caused the ball to stop moving?

3. Make an **inference.** What would happen to the ball if there was no friction to slow it down or no object in the way to stop it? Explain.

? Inquire Further

What could you do to make the quarter stay on the card when you flick the card off the cup? How could you keep the ball in the cup when you stop the cup? Develop a plan to answer these or other questions you may have.

Exploring Weight

The mass of an object is the amount of matter it contains. An object's mass is the same anywhere in the universe. However, an object's weight depends on gravity. The force of gravity is different on the moon than it is on the earth, and so is an object's weight. In this chapter, you will learn about weight. How can you find out whether one object weighs more than another?

Work Together

Pick 5 small objects in your classroom (such as a box of crayons, a stapler, a large marker) and compare their weights.

1. Pick up the objects and estimate which is the heaviest, which is the next heaviest, and so on.

2. Arrange the objects in order from heaviest to lightest.

3. Now use a balance. Compare the weights of the objects you chose. Did you arrange the objects in the correct order?

Talk About It!

1. Which weighs more, a dollar bill or a quarter? Does the larger object always weigh more? Explain.

2. Did any of your objects weigh the same? How could you tell?

Materials
- balance
- small classroom objects

Did You Know?
An object weighs $\frac{1}{6}$ as much on the moon as on the earth, but its mass stays the same.

▼ *Which of these two objects is heavier?*

You will learn:
- what makes things move.
- how gravity affects motion.
- how friction affects motion.

Glossary

Glossary

force (fôrs), a push or a pull on an object that can cause it to change motion

Lesson 1

How Do Forces Affect Motion?

VROOM! Up, down, and around you go on a roller coaster. **EEEE!** You scream as you feel yourself being pushed and pulled from side to side. You're in motion!

Moving Objects

The dog in the picture is using force, a pull, to move the child. A **force** is a push or a pull on an object that can cause it to change motion. Forces also make roller coasters go up and down.

Forces can cause objects to start moving, speed up, slow down, stop, or change direction. For example, your friend kicks a soccer ball to you. You kick it back. You've just used a force to change the direction of the soccer ball. The harder you kick the soccer ball, the farther it will go. Heavier objects, such as bowling balls, need more force to move them.

When the dog pulls the girl, it is using force. ▼

Force of Gravity

Have you ever gone down the slope of a roller coaster and felt as if you were falling? You felt the effects of gravity. **Gravity** is the force that pulls two objects toward one another because of their mass. Gravity pulls you toward the center of the earth. The roller coaster cars in the picture are being pulled down toward the earth by the force of gravity.

You can see the force of gravity at work. Think about the last time you tossed a ball up in the air. What happened? The ball came down because the force of gravity pulled it toward the earth. No matter how high or how hard you toss the ball, it will always come back down.

Gravity is a force that can be measured. How much do you weigh? When you step on a scale to find out, the scale measures the force of gravity between you and the earth. Your weight is a measure of the pull of the earth's gravity on your body. How much you weigh depends on the mass of your body. The greater the mass of your body, the greater the pull of gravity on your body and the more you weigh.

Glossary

gravity (grav′ə tē), a force that pulls any two objects toward one another, such as you toward the center of the earth

Gravity is the force pulling the roller coaster cars toward the earth. ▶

Glossary

Glossary

inertia (in ėr′shə), the tendency of a moving object to stay in motion or a resting object to stay at rest

Force of Friction

History of Science

Many years ago, the scientist Isaac Newton made a discovery about moving objects. He learned that a moving object will continue moving in a straight line until a force causes it to slow down or stop. Newton also discovered that an object not moving, or at rest, will stay at rest until a force, such as a push or pull, moves it. The tendency of an object to keep moving in a straight line or to stay at rest is called **inertia.** All objects have inertia.

The children in the picture are in motion on in-line skates. The children used a pushing force to overcome inertia and begin moving. They will continue to move until another force slows them down or stops them. When the children stop, they will stay at rest until a force moves them.

These children will stay in motion until a force slows them down or stops them. ▼

Imagine that you find a soccer ball on the ground. The soccer ball is at rest and will stay at rest until a force acts on it to move it. You kick the soccer ball. You have applied a force and the soccer ball begins to move. The soccer ball will keep moving until another force stops it.

As the soccer ball moves over the ground, the ground rubs against the ball. The rubbing of the ground slows the ball down. The ball continues to slow down until it stops.

The ground rubbing against the soccer ball caused friction. **Friction** is a force that slows down or stops moving objects such as a soccer ball in motion. Friction occurs when two objects rub against each other. Rub your hands together. Do your hands get warm? You are causing friction. Friction changes the energy of rubbing your hands into heat energy.

As the children move on their in-line skates, such as the one in the picture, the wheels rub against the ground. The rubbing causes friction. If the children stop pushing the skates, the friction slows them down. Using the brake causes more friction. The friction will slow them down or stop them.

Glossary

Glossary

friction (frik′shən), a force that slows the motion of moving objects

When two things rub together, they cause friction. The brakes on this in-line skate rub on the ground, causing friction. ▼

Lesson 1 Review

1. What are two effects that forces can have on motion?

2. How is a ball tossed in the air like a roller coaster car rolling down a track?

3. Describe how friction affects the motion of an object.

4. **Weight**
   Arrange the following objects in order from lightest to heaviest: bowling ball, roller coaster, soccer ball, astronaut.

Reducing Friction

Process Skills

Process Skills

- observing
- estimating and measuring
- inferring

Materials

- safety goggles
- glue
- spool
- cardboard circle with hole
- smooth, level surface
- masking tape
- half-meter stick
- balloon
- sinker

Getting Ready

You can find out how air can reduce friction by making a hovercraft.

Follow This Procedure

❶ Make a chart like the one shown. Use your chart to record your measurements.

	Distance of movement		
	Trial 1	Trial 2	Trial 3
No balloon			
With balloon			
With balloon and sinker			

❷ Put on your safety goggles. Glue the spool to the cardboard on top of the hole. Make sure the holes line up. Use enough glue to assure that no air can escape from between the spool and cardboard (Photo A). Allow the glue to dry. This is your hovercraft.

❸ Place the hovercraft, spool side up, on a smooth, level surface. This could be a desk, table, or the floor. Mark a starting point with tape. Give the hovercraft a small push with your hand. **Observe** its motion and **measure** how far it goes. Record your measurement. Repeat two more times.

❹ Blow up the balloon and twist the end to keep the air from escaping.

 Safety Note Do not overinflate the balloon. Never inhale from a balloon while inflating it.

Photo A

Photo B

5 Keep the end twisted closed. Have a partner hold the balloon while you stretch the opening of the balloon over the top of the spool. Be sure to center the balloon opening over the hole in the spool (Photo B).

6 Repeat step 3 but untwist the balloon before you push the hovercraft.

7 Test to see how far the hovercraft travels with a sinker taped near to the spool. Repeat two more times. Try to push the hovercraft with the same force each time.

Interpret Your Results

1. Friction causes the hovercraft to slow down and stop. What can you **infer** about the friction between the hovercraft and the surface when air from the balloon was forced between them?

2. What can you infer about the friction between the hovercraft and the surface when you added the sinker?

 **Inquire Further**

How would the hovercraft work on other surfaces? Develop a plan to answer this or other questions you may have.

Self-Assessment

- I followed instructions to make a hovercraft.
- I **observed** and **measured** the distance the hovercraft moved.
- I recorded my observations and measurements.
- I made an **inference** about friction when air was forced between the hovercraft and the surface.
- I made an inference about friction when the sinker was added to the hovercraft.

What's the Big Idea?

You will learn:
- what potential energy is.
- what kinetic energy is.
- about other forms of energy that affect motion.

Glossary

energy (en′ər jē), the ability to do work

potential (pə ten′shəl) **energy,** energy that an object has because of position

How Does Energy Affect Motion?

 YIPPIE! Back and forth you swing. Higher and higher you go as you lean forward and tilt back. **WHEE!** Did you know that swinging uses energy?

Potential Energy

You have probably heard people talk about energy many times, but what is energy? In science, **energy** is the ability to do work. You use energy every time you do work—or move an object. Energy has many forms and can change from one form to another.

Did you ever sit at the top of a slide, such as the one in the picture, waiting to go down? While you sat at the top of the slide, you had potential energy.

Potential energy is energy that an object has because of position. Find the child in the picture on the next page who is at the highest point on the swing set. The swing has the most potential energy at this point. The higher the swing goes up, the faster it will come down and the farther it will move forward.

◀ *The boy has potential energy because he is at the top of the slide.*

Kinetic Energy

When anything moves, it has a form of energy called kinetic energy. **Kinetic energy** is the energy of motion. Look again at the children on the swings. The swing moving downward has kinetic energy. As it goes back up, the kinetic energy becomes potential energy, or energy of position. Potential energy changes to kinetic energy and back to potential energy with each swing.

Glossary

kinetic (ki net′ik) **energy,** energy of motion

Glossary

Potential energy changes to kinetic energy as the swing moves down. Kinetic energy changes to potential energy as the swing moves up. ▼

Glossary

Glossary

mechanical (mə kan′ə kəl) **energy,** the kind of energy an object has because it can move or because it is moving

chemical (kem′ə kəl) **energy,** energy that comes from chemical changes

electrical (i lek′trə kəl) **energy,** energy that comes from the flow of electricity

Other Forms of Energy

Kinetic and potential energy may take different forms. Mechanical, chemical, and electrical energy are forms of energy. Light, heat, and sound are other forms of energy. Think about the last time you plugged in your radio, turned the propeller of a model airplane, or put a battery into a game. Each of these objects uses energy. Look at the pictures to see how energy affects motion.

◀ *Mechanical energy is the energy an object has because it can move or because it is moving. Mechanical energy can be potential energy or kinetic energy. When the bicycle moves, potential mechanical energy is changed to kinetic mechanical energy.*

Chemical energy is a kind of potential energy you find in things like gasoline and other fuels. The battery that runs the toy in the picture has potential chemical energy. All matter has potential chemical energy. Some matter, such as the foods you eat, can release their chemical energy. Your body uses the chemical energy from the food to grow and move. ▶

Lesson 2 Review

1. What is potential energy? Give an example.

2. When does an object have kinetic energy? Give an example.

3. List three other forms of energy. Describe how each one affects motion.

4. **Main Idea**
   What is the main idea of the caption for chemical energy on page B44?

▲ **Electrical energy** is a form of energy that comes from the flow of electricity. Electrical energy moves this merry-go-round.

Changing Forms of Energy

Process Skills

- observing
- measuring

Materials

- safety goggles
- scissors
- 2 rubber bands
- sinker
- cylindrical cardboard box
- half-meter stick
- masking tape

Getting Ready

In this activity you will observe changes in potential and kinetic energy.

Follow This Procedure

① Make a chart like the one shown. Use your chart to record your measurements.

	Distance box rolls
First roll	
Second roll	
Third roll	

② Put on your safety goggles. Use scissors to cut each rubber band into one long piece.

③ Thread one end of each rubber band through the hole at the top of the sinker (Photo A).

Photo A

④ Remove the lid from the box. Thread the ends of one rubber band through the holes in the inside bottom of the box. Pull the ends of the rubber band through the holes until the sinker is in the center of the box. Tie the ends of the rubber band together on the outside of the bottom of the box (Photo B).

Photo B

Photo C

⑤ Have a partner hold the bottom of the box. Thread the ends of the other rubber band through the lid of the box. Place the lid back onto the box. Pull the ends of the rubber band tight so that the sinker does not touch the side of the box. Tie the ends of the rubber band together. Photo C shows the completed device with the top removed so you can see how it is assembled.

⑥ Attach 1 m of masking tape to a table or the floor. Place the box on its side at one end of the tape.

⑦ Push the box gently so that it rolls along the tape strip. **Observe** the movement of the box. Ask a partner to mark how far the box rolls before it stops and begins to roll back to you. **Measure** how far it rolled. Record your measurement.

⑧ Repeat step 7 two more times, pushing the box a little harder each time.

Interpret Your Results

1. Describe how the potential and kinetic energy changed as you pushed the box and as it rolled back to you.

2. How did the force of the push affect the box's potential and kinetic energy?

 **Inquire Further**

What would happen if you did not stop the box when it rolled back to you? Develop a plan to answer this or other questions you may have.

Self-Assessment

- I followed instructions to make a device showing changes in potential and kinetic energy.
- I **observed** the movement of the box.
- I **measured** how far the box rolled when pushed with different amounts of force.
- I recorded my measurements.
- I described how the potential and kinetic energy of the box changed.

You will learn:

- what work is.
- how simple machines affect motion.
- what compound and complex machines are.

Lesson 3

How Are Work and Motion Related?

Homework! Housework! Yard work! **WHEW!** Do you ever wonder what the word *work* means? How do you know you are doing work?

Work

You use energy to work every day. When you lift a glass of milk or pull open a door, you have done work.

Two things must happen for work to be done. A force must act on an object and the force must have enough energy to make the object move. **Work** is done when a force moves an object. You learned that pushes and pulls are forces. When pushes and pulls move objects, work is done.

The woman in the picture is using a force, a push, to move the swing. When the swing moves in the direction of the force, work is done.

The amount of work you do depends on how much force you use and how far the object moves. The woman does more work if she pushes harder and the swing moves higher. The woman would do even more work if the child were heavier. She would need to use more force to move the swing.

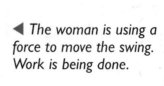

◀ *The woman is using a force to move the swing. Work is being done.*

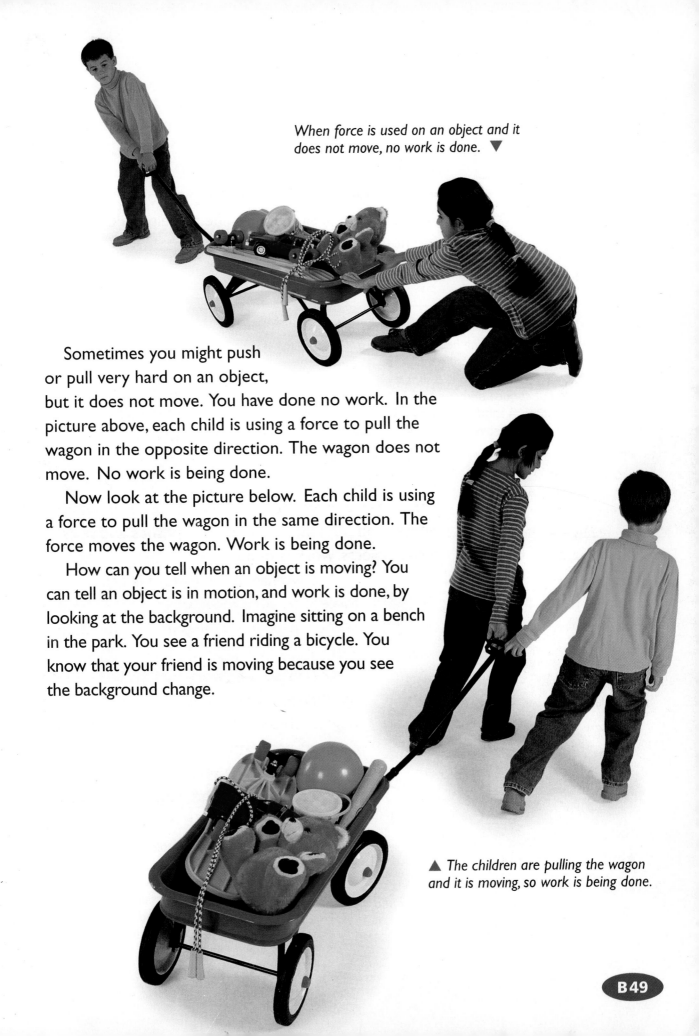

When force is used on an object and it does not move, no work is done. ▼

Sometimes you might push or pull very hard on an object, but it does not move. You have done no work. In the picture above, each child is using a force to pull the wagon in the opposite direction. The wagon does not move. No work is being done.

Now look at the picture below. Each child is using a force to pull the wagon in the same direction. The force moves the wagon. Work is being done.

How can you tell when an object is moving? You can tell an object is in motion, and work is done, by looking at the background. Imagine sitting on a bench in the park. You see a friend riding a bicycle. You know that your friend is moving because you see the background change.

▲ *The children are pulling the wagon and it is moving, so work is being done.*

Glossary

simple machine
(sim/pəl mə shēn/),
a machine made of one
or two parts

Simple Machines

Suppose you want to help build a tree house for your community. What things will you need? You will definitely need tools. A tool is a machine that makes work easier. A **simple machine** is a machine made of one or two parts. Notice that everyone in the picture is using a simple machine to help build the tree house. Read to find out about each of the simple machines.

Inclined Plane

The child below is easily moving heavy materials in a wheelbarrow by using an inclined plane. An inclined plane is a simple machine with a flat surface and one end higher than the other. A ramp is an inclined plane. It makes moving heavy items easier.

Wheel and Axle

The wheelbarrow is rolling on a wheel and axle. A wheel and axle is a simple machine made of a wheel attached to a rod. As the wheel turns, it turns the rod.

Wedge

A wedge is a simple machine that has slanted sides. A nail is a wedge. The slanted sides of the nail make it easier to pound the nail into the wood. The adult is about to use a nail to hold wood together.

Pulley

This child is using a pulley to raise materials up to the tree house. A pulley is a simple machine that uses a rope and a wheel. As the child pulls down on one end of the rope, the other end of the rope pulls the materials up.

Screw

This child is using a screw to put up the sign. A screw is a simple machine that holds materials together. A screw is an inclined plane wrapped around a rod. The inclined plane makes the screw easier to put into the wood. The grooves also help hold the screw in the wood.

Lever

The screwdriver is an example of a simple machine called a lever. The edge of the paint can is part of this lever too. Notice that the child puts one end of the screwdriver under the lid of the can. The edge of the can supports this lever. Therefore, the edge of the can is the fulcrum for this lever. To open the can, the child pushes down on one end of the screwdriver. The fulcrum changes the direction of the force, and the other end of the screwdriver pushes up on the lid.

Glossary

compound machine
(kom′pound mə shēn′),
a machine made of two
or more simple machines

▲ *Garden shears*

Compound and Complex Machines

A **compound machine** is made up of two or more simple machines. The simple machines that make up the garden shears shown in the picture are a lever and two wedges. The cutting edges of the blades are wedges. The pin is the fulcrum that changes the direction of the force on the garden shears. When the handles of the shears are pulled in one direction, the blades of the shears move in the opposite direction.

The hand mower below is also a compound machine. Notice the simple machines that make up the hand mower. The handle is a lever. Each blade is a wedge that cuts grass. The mower rolls on two wheels and an axle. All these simple machines together make up a compound machine—the hand mower.

On the next page, notice the picture of another compound machine—a bicycle. Look at the pictures to see what kinds of simple machines make up a bicycle.

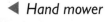

◀ *Hand mower*

Parts of a Compound Machine

Wheel and Axle
The pedals are connected by cranks to the big sprocket. The big sprocket is the big-toothed wheel that is turned by the pedals and cranks.

Screws
A bicycle has many screws that hold the parts of the bicycle together.

Levers
The hand brakes on the bicycle are levers.

Wheel and Axle
The small sprocket, or small-toothed wheel, and the rear wheel on the bicycle are another wheel and axle. When the sprocket turns, the rear wheel turns. When the back wheel turns, it makes the front wheel turn, and the bicycle moves.

Wheel and Axle
Together, the pedals, cranks, and big sprocket make up a wheel and axle.

Glossary

complex machine
(kom′pleks mə shēn′),
a machine made of many
simple and compound
machines

Motorcycles, cars, and robots are complex machines. A **complex machine** is a machine made up of many simple and compound machines. The car engine in the picture is a complex machine. Most complex machines are run by electricity or fuels.

A car engine is made up of many moving parts. ▶

Lesson 3 Review

1. When is work done? Give an example.

2. How many parts does a simple machine have? Describe a situation in which a simple machine can be used to do work.

3. How is a compound machine similar to a simple machine? How are complex machines different from compound machines?

4. **Main Idea**
   What is the main idea of the paragraph at the top of this page?

Experimenting with Pulleys

Materials

- dowel
- 2 desks
- masking tape
- metric ruler
- lump of clay
- measuring cup
- water
- plastic bottle with handle
- string
- spring scale

Process Skills

- formulating questions and hypotheses
- identifying and controlling variables
- experimenting
- estimating and measuring
- collecting and interpreting data
- communicating

State the Problem

How does the number of pulleys used affect the effort needed to lift an object?

Formulate Your Hypothesis

If you increase the number of pulleys used, will you need to use more, less, or the same effort to lift an object? Write your hypothesis.

Identify and Control the Variables

The number of pulleys used is the variable you can change. In Trial 1 you will lift an object with a single pulley system. In Trial 2 you will lift the object with a double pulley system. In Trial 3 you will use a triple pulley system. The mass lifted must remain the same for each trial.

Test Your Hypothesis

Follow these steps to perform an experiment.

❶ Make a chart like the one on the next page. Use your chart to record your observations.

❷ Place the dowel between two desks and tape the ends down to the desk. Stick a ruler in clay on the floor to stand it up. Place the ruler under the dowel (Photo A).

Photo A

Continued ➜

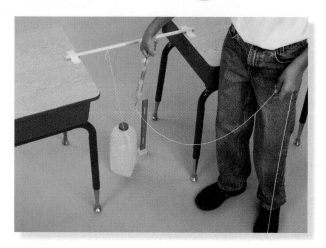

Photo B

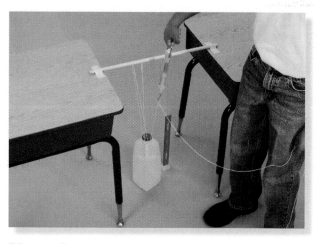

Photo C

❸ Pour about 200 mL of water into the bottle. Put the cap on the bottle. Tie one end of the string to the dowel. Make a single pulley system by passing the string behind and through to the front of the handle of the bottle. Tie the end of the string to the spring scale.

❹ Pull up on the spring scale to raise the bottle 10 cm from the floor (Photo B). Notice the effort shown on the spring scale. **Collect data** by recording the **measurement** in your chart.

❺ Untie the spring scale. Pass the end of the string over the top of the dowel from the front. Then pass the string behind and through to the front of the bottle handle. Tie the end of the string to the spring scale. Now you have a double pulley system.

❻ Repeat step 4 (Photo C).

❼ Repeat step 5 to make a triple pulley system. Then repeat step 4 one more time (Photo D).

Collect Your Data

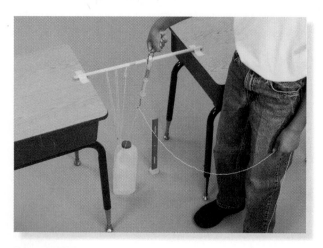

Photo D

Pulley system	Effort to raise bottle 10 cm
Single	
Double	
Triple	

Interpret Your Data

1. Label a piece of grid paper as shown. Use the data from your chart to make a graph on your grid paper.

2. Study your graph. Describe what happened to the effort required to lift the bottle as you added pulleys. Did the effort increase, decrease, or remain the same?

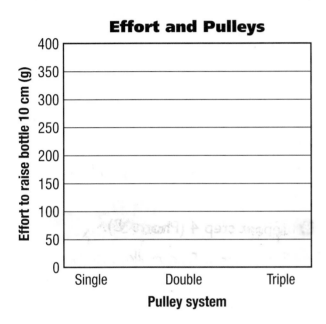

Effort and Pulleys

State Your Conclusion

How do your results compare with your hypothesis? **Communicate** your results. How does the number of pulleys used affect the effort needed to lift an object?

Inquire Further

Would adding another pulley system make lifting the load easier? Develop a plan to answer this or other questions you may have.

Self-Assessment

- I made a **hypothesis** about the effects of pulleys on the effort needed to lift an object.
- I **identified** and **controlled variables** and I followed instructions to perform an **experiment** with pulleys.
- I **measured** the effort needed to lift a bottle with pulleys.
- I **collected** and **interpreted data** by recording measurements and making a graph.
- I **communicated** by stating my conclusion.

Chapter 2 Review

Chapter Main Ideas

Lesson 1

• A force is a push or a pull that can make an object move.

• Gravity is the force that pulls two objects together and pulls you toward the center of the earth.

• Friction slows down or stops objects that are in motion.

Lesson 2

• Potential energy is energy that an object has because of its position.

• Kinetic energy is the energy an object has because of its motion.

• Mechanical, electrical, and chemical energy are forms of energy that can affect motion.

Lesson 3

• When a force moves an object, work is done.

• Simple machines are tools with one or two parts that are used to make work easier.

  • Compound machines are made up of two or more simple machines; complex machines are made of many simple and compound machines.

Reviewing Science Words and Concepts

Write the letter of the word or phrase that best completes each sentence.

a. chemical energy

b. complex machine

c. compound machine

d. electrical energy

e. energy

f. force

g. friction

h. gravity

i. inertia

j. kinetic energy

k. mechanical energy

l. potential energy

m. simple machine

n. work

1. A roller coaster car goes up and down because it is moved by a ____.

2. The force of ____ is what pulls a roller coaster car to the earth.

3. The tendency for an object to stay in motion until a force stops it is called ____.

4. When you apply the brakes on your bike, the brakes rub against the wheel and cause ____.

5. You can do work because you have potential ____.

6. As a child moves down a slide, ____ becomes energy of motion.

7. When you throw a ball, potential energy becomes ____.

8. A bicycle in motion has kinetic energy in the form of ____.

9. A battery has a kind of potential energy called ____.

10. A merry-go-round can be moved by the flow of electricity, or ____.

11. If you kick a soccer ball and it moves, you know that you have done ____.

12. A wheel and axle is a ____ that has two parts.

13. A bicycle is a ____ that is made up of several simple machines.

14. The engine of a car is a ____.

Explaining Science

Write a sentence or sentences to answer these questions.

1. What did Isaac Newton discover about moving objects?

2. What is the difference between kinetic energy and potential energy?

3. How do you know when work is done?

Using Skills

1. Use what you learned about **weight** to arrange the following objects in order from heaviest to lightest: pencil, bicycle, soccer ball, feather.

2. Suppose a small child and an adult are climbing a hill at the same speed. **Apply** what you have learned to decide who is doing more work. Explain your answer.

3. Observe your arms and legs. Decide which simple machine your arms and legs are similar to.

Critical Thinking

1. A child has a box of comic books she got from a garage sale. She brought the books home in a wagon, but she can't carry the box up the steps into the house. **Make a decision** about which simple machine she can construct that will help her get the box of comics up the steps.

2. A boy hits a ball as hard as he can. The ball bounces along the field and comes to a stop without anyone touching it. **Make** an **inference** about what forces caused the ball to slow down and stop.

3. What changes in forms of energy take place when you walk to school? **Communicate** your explanation.

It's For You!

Imagine what life would be like without electricity and magnetism. No phone calls, CD players, or headphones. What would you miss the most?

Chapter 3
Electricity and Magnetism

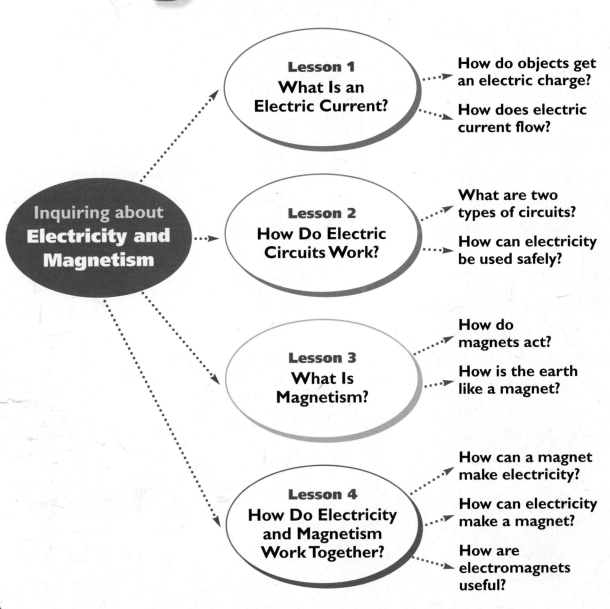

Inquiring about Electricity and Magnetism

Lesson 1
What Is an Electric Current?
- How do objects get an electric charge?
- How does electric current flow?

Lesson 2
How Do Electric Circuits Work?
- What are two types of circuits?
- How can electricity be used safely?

Lesson 3
What Is Magnetism?
- How do magnets act?
- How is the earth like a magnet?

Lesson 4
How Do Electricity and Magnetism Work Together?
- How can a magnet make electricity?
- How can electricity make a magnet?
- How are electromagnets useful?

Copy the chapter graphic organizer onto your own paper. This organizer shows you what the whole chapter is all about. As you read the lessons and do the activities, look for answers to the questions and write them on your organizer.

Exploring Electric Charge

Process Skills

- observing
- inferring
- communicating

Materials

- safety goggles
- balloon
- string
- unflavored gelatin powder
- dark construction paper
- wool cloth

Explore

❶ Put on your safety goggles. Inflate a balloon. Hold the opening closed while another student ties a string tightly around the neck of the balloon so no air can escape.

❷ Pour some of the gelatin powder onto the center of the construction paper.

❸ Bring the balloon very close to the gelatin powder, as shown in the photo. Record and draw your **observations.**

❹ Give the balloon an electric charge by rubbing it on the wool cloth for about 30 seconds. Then repeat step 3.

❺ Now rub the powder back onto the construction paper. Rub your hand over the entire surface of the balloon. Then repeat step 3.

Reflect

1. What cause and effect did you observe?

2. Make an **inference.** How can a balloon become charged and uncharged? Explain your answer. **Communicate.** Discuss your ideas with the class.

? Inquire Further

What happens when a charged balloon is brought near other materials?
    Develop a plan to answer this or other questions you may have.

Identifying Cause and Effect

In the first lesson, *What Is an Electric Current?*, you will find examples of cause and effect. A cause makes something happen. An effect is the outcome or result. As you read the lesson, look for effects. Then ask yourself what caused the effects to happen.

Reading Vocabulary

cause (koz), a person, thing, or event that makes something happen

effect (ə fekt′), whatever is produced by a cause; a result

Example

One way to better understand the activity and the lesson is to make a chart like this one. Then look for the causes of each of the effects listed in the chart. Write the causes in your chart.

Causes	Effects
? →	A balloon gains a negative charge.
? →	Two charged balloons repel each other.
? →	Two charged balloons attract each other.

Talk About It!

1. What is the difference between a cause and an effect?

2. What caused the gelatin powder to jump to the balloon in the activity *Exploring Electric Charge?*

B 63

You will learn:
- how objects get an electric charge.
- how electric current flows.

Lesson 1

What Is an Electric Current?

 ZAP! Your friend shuffles her feet and walks toward you across the rug. She touches you. **OUCH!** You get an electric shock. What caused this to happen?

Electric Charge

If you rub two objects together, negative electric charges can move from one object to the other. Objects, such as balloons, people, and rugs, are all made up of matter. Matter is made up of tiny particles, and each of these particles is made of even smaller bits of matter. Some of the smaller bits have a negative (−) electric charge. Other bits have a positive (+) charge, and some have no charge.

Usually, objects have a balance of negative and positive charges. But this can change. Your friend rubbed the rug with her feet. The rubbing caused some bits of matter with negative charges to rub off from the rug onto her.

Before she rubbed the rug, your friend's body and clothing had an equal, or balanced, number of positive and negative charges. The more she rubbed her feet on the rug, the greater the number of negative charges she picked up.

When one person or object has more negative charges than positive charges, the extra negative charges move toward the positive charges in the other person or object. ▼

▲ These balloons have different charges. The positive and negative charges attract each other.

▲ These two balloons each have a negative charge. Like charges repel, or push apart.

Meanwhile, you sat there. Your body had a balanced number of negative and positive charges. Notice the different numbers of negative and positive charges on each child in the picture on page B64. When your friend reached toward you, the extra negative charges on her flowed toward the positive charges on you. Zap! You felt an electric shock. She felt the shock too.

What else can happen when an electric charge builds up in things? The electric charges in two objects can cause either a pulling or a pushing force. Look at the pictures on this page to see what happens when objects have like and different charges.

When two objects have different charges, they pull together. When two objects have the same charge, they repel each other, or push apart. If you rub two balloons on your sleeve, negative charges rub onto the balloons. If you hold them each up by a string, the like charges will push the balloons apart.

▲ Suppose you held up these two balloons. Would their charges push them apart or pull them together? Explain why.

Glossary

Glossary

resistance
(ri zis′təns), a measure of how much a material opposes the flow of electric current and changes electric current into heat energy

conductor
(kən duk′tər), a material through which electric current passes easily

insulator
(in′sə lā′tər), a material through which electric current does not pass easily

Electric Current

Electric current is the flow of negative charges through matter. You make small electric charges when you drag your feet on the rug, touch someone, and cause a spark to jump. However, these charges only last a moment. To run a VCR, light bulb, or computer, you need an electric current that continues to flow. In the case of the spark, the charges flow through the air or the person or thing you touch. In the case of a VCR or a light bulb, the electric current flows through metal wires to these appliances.

At home, you plug machines into an outlet or turn on a switch. A strong electric current flows. This current travels to your house through wires from an electric power generator. A battery, such as the ones in the picture, can also provide an electric current to light a bulb or run a radio. However, electric current can only flow when it has a closed path, or a closed circuit, to flow through.

The diagram on the next page shows how electric current flows in a closed circuit. Trace the path of the electric current beginning at the battery.

Battery

Have you noticed the "+" and "−" marks on batteries? The "+" end of the battery has a positive charge. The "−" end has a negative electric charge. When the battery is in a closed circuit, the negative charges flow out from the negative end of the battery, through the wires, and back to the battery's positive end. Follow the path of the closed circuit on the next page. ▶

A Closed Circuit

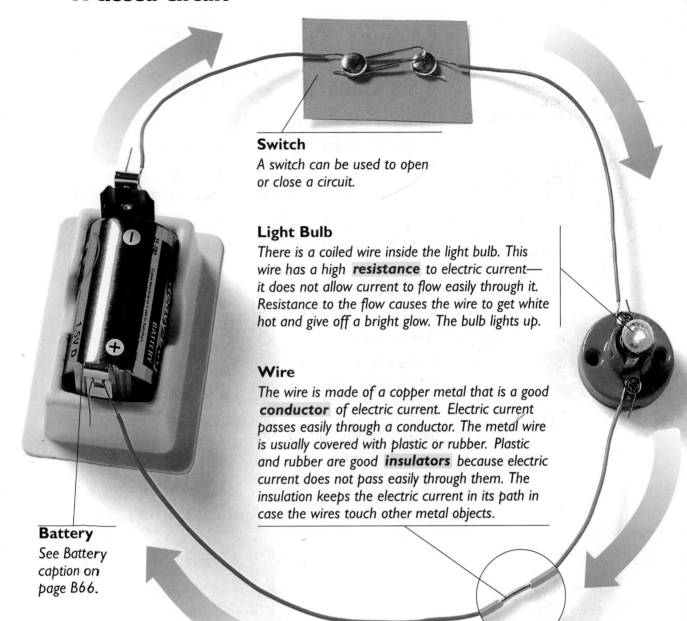

Switch
A switch can be used to open
or close a circuit.

Light Bulb
There is a coiled wire inside the light bulb. This
wire has a high **resistance** to electric current—
it does not allow current to flow easily through it.
Resistance to the flow causes the wire to get white
hot and give off a bright glow. The bulb lights up.

Wire
The wire is made of a copper metal that is a good
conductor of electric current. Electric current
passes easily through a conductor. The metal wire
is usually covered with plastic or rubber. Plastic
and rubber are good **insulators** because electric
current does not pass easily through them. The
insulation keeps the electric current in its path in
case the wires touch other metal objects.

Battery
See Battery
caption on
page B66.

Lesson 1 Review

1. How does an object get an electric charge?

2. What happens to an electric current when a
   circuit is closed?

3. **Cause and Effect**
   What causes the bulb to light in a
   closed circuit?

You will learn:

- about two types of circuits.
- how electricity can be used safely.

Lesson 2

How Do Electric Circuits Work?

Light! Color! Sound! Flip a switch, and your computer comes alive. Because electric current flows through wires in circuits in your home or school, you can learn by computer or surf the internet. Visit the website at www.sfscience.com.

Electric Circuits

You know that electric current flows only through a closed circuit. As long as the path is unbroken, the current flows. To break a closed circuit, you turn off a switch or remove a part of the path. When electric current does not travel through a circuit, the circuit is open. Just think! Every time you turn off a light, you open a closed circuit.

◀ **Series Circuit**
The bulbs and wires make one single path. Use your finger to trace the path of the current through the circuit.

A series circuit is one way to build a closed electric circuit. In a **series circuit,** several light bulbs or other appliances are connected in one path. Find the series circuit in the picture on page B68. Notice that there is only one possible path for the electric current to follow.

In a series circuit, all the parts must be "on" to complete the circuit. If even one light bulb is missing or burned out, the whole circuit won't work. If your classroom had a series circuit, the computer would shut off every time someone turned off the lights!

Another way to build a closed electric circuit is a parallel circuit. In a **parallel circuit,** each bulb has its own path. Find the parallel circuit in the picture.

The circuits in your home and school are parallel circuits. You plug in your desk lamp. This puts the desk lamp on one parallel circuit. Your radio might run on the same parallel circuit. With a parallel circuit, you can turn off the desk lamp and the radio can stay on. Parallel circuits allow electric items to be turned on and off separately.

Glossary

series circuit
(sir′ēz sėr′kit), a circuit that connects several objects one after another so that the current flows in a single path

parallel circuit
(par′ə lel sėr′kit), a circuit that connects several objects in a way that the current for each object has its own path

Glossary

Parallel Circuit ▶
If a bulb is burned out, the circuit is still closed. The current can still flow. Use your finger to trace two ways to make a closed circuit.

Using Electricity Safely

⚠️ Electricity must always be used with great care. A strong electric current traveling into your body can be very dangerous. The shock can cause bad burns to your body, or even stop your heart! Electric current also produces heat and can start fires. To use electricity safely, follow the guidelines on these pages.

◀ **Unload That Outlet!**

Don't plug too many appliances into one outlet. Too much current traveling through one circuit can cause an overload. The wires inside a wall can get too hot and start a fire. Using a special safety power strip can help prevent overloading a circuit.

Replace That Cord!

Frayed, cut, or broken electric cords cannot protect you from electric current. Electricity can travel to your body through the break. Worn wires can also overheat and cause a fire. ▶

▲ Unplug Those Appliances!

Be sure to unplug your hair dryer or curling iron when you finish using it. It could cause a fire.

Move Those Papers!

Make sure that papers and other objects that can burn are moved away from an electric heater before it is turned on. Papers, curtains, and other objects that can burn might catch fire from the heater. ▶

▲ Keep It Dry!

Water conducts electricity. So can your body. Never touch electric appliances or cords when you are wet. Never use electric appliances around water. Make sure counters, sinks, and floors are dry.

Lesson 2 Review

1. How is a series circuit different from a parallel circuit?

2. Name three ways to use electricity safely.

3. **Cause and Effect**
   Write about how the unsafe use of electricity can cause harm.

Comparing Series and Parallel Circuits

Process Skills

- predicting
- observing
- inferring

Materials

- safety goggles
- D-cell battery
- battery holder
- 2 flashlight bulbs and holders
- 4 pieces of insulated wire with ends stripped

Getting Ready

You can safely investigate circuits using electricity from a D-cell battery.

Look at the pictures of circuits on the next page. You will need to study these carefully to complete the activity.

Follow This Procedure

❶ Make a chart like the one shown. Use your chart to record your predictions and observations.

	Predictions	Observations
One bulb removed from series circuit		
One bulb removed from parallel circuit		

❷ Put on your safety goggles. Look at the picture of the series circuit (Photo A). With your finger, trace the path that electricity takes through the circuit.

❸ Both bulbs should be on a strong. What will happen if you remove one of the bulbs? Record your **prediction.**

❹ Remove one of the bulbs and record your **observation.** Replace the bulb, then disconnect the circuit.

❺ Look at the picture of the parallel circuit (Photo B). With your finger, trace the different paths that electricity can take through the circuit. Make a drawing of the circuit. Build the parallel circuit as shown.

❻ Repeat steps 3 and 4.

Self-Monitoring

Do I have questions to ask before I continue?

Photo A
Series circuit

Photo B
Parallel circuit

Interpret Your Results

1. Look at your draw~~ing~~ ~~s~~ries
~~circuit and th~~ ~~w~~

2. We~~re~~ ~~o~~ctions about
removing a bulb from each circuit
correct? Explain h~~ow~~ ~~s~~ries circuits and
parallel circuits are alike and different.

3. You may have noticed that the bulbs
were dim in the series circuit and
bright in the parallel circuit. Make an
inference. What would happen to the
brightness of the bulbs if you added
another bulb to the series circuit?
Explain.

Inquire Further

Does the number of bulbs in a series
circuit or a parallel circuit affect the
brightness of the bulbs? Develop a plan
to answer this or other questions you
may have.

Self-Assessment

- I followed instructions and used
  pictures to draw and construct a series
  circuit and a parallel circuit.
- I recorded my **predictions** and
  observations.
- I drew arrows to show the path of
  electricity through each circuit.
- I explained how parallel and series circuits
  are alike and different.
- I made an **inference** about the brightness
  of bulbs connected in a series circuit.

B 73

You will learn:
- how magnets act.
- how the earth is like a magnet.

Lesson 3

What Is Magnetism?

You notice a note on the refrigerator door. Then you pull open the door. **Guess what?** You just found two magnets. One magnet holds the note on the metal door. Another magnet, hidden inside the door, holds the door closed.

How Magnets Act

A **magnet** is anything that will attract, or pull, iron, steel, and certain other metals to it. **Magnetism** is the pulling or pushing force that exists ar~~ound a~~ magnet. When you place a magnet near iron ~~or steel~~, the two objects pull toward each other wit~~h a stron~~g force. Because a refrigerator door is made partly of steel, a magnet will easily stick to it.

A **magnetic field** is the space around a magnet where magnetism acts. Magnetic force is invisible, but you can use tiny pieces of iron to see the magnetic field formed by magnetic force. Find the magnetic field in the picture below.

The tiny pieces of iron line up along the lines of magnetic force. The iron pieces cluster around the poles, where the magnetic force is the greatest. ▶

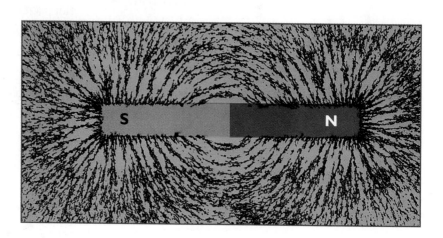

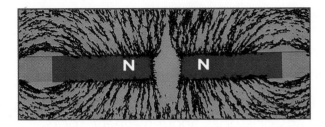

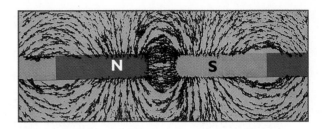

▲ Like poles push apart. Here the like ends of two magnets are near each other. The magnetic forces repel, or push away from, each other. The magnets push apart.

▲ Unlike poles pull together. Here the unlike ends of two magnets are near each other. The magnetic forces attract, or pull strongly together. The magnets may snap together.

The magnets shown here have two ends called **poles.** If these magnets are allowed to swing freely, one pole, the north-seeking pole, points north. Sometimes it is marked N. The south-seeking pole points south. Sometimes it is marked S.

How else do a magnet's poles act? You know that like electric charges push away from each other and that unlike charges pull strongly toward each other. Magnets act the same way. The pictures above show what happens when like and unlike poles are placed near each other.

A magnet's poles also act in another way. Look at the picture below. Which parts of the magnet pick up the most paper clips? You can see that the magnetic force is strongest at a magnet's poles.

Glossary

pole (pōl), a place on a magnet where magnetism is strongest

Glossary

More paper clips stick to the ends, or poles, of the magnet. ▶

Glossary

compass (kum′pəs), a small magnet that can turn freely

▲ *The lodestone attracts the metal nails.*

The Earth: A Giant Magnet

In ancient times, people noticed certain rocks that pulled together or pushed apart. These rocks, such as the one in the picture, are called lodestones. The early Greeks had legends, or stories, about magnetic rocks. One story was about a shepherd. The legend claimed that the iron tacks in his sandals stuck to a rock when he stepped on it. Another legend claimed that a magnetic mountain could pull nails out of wooden ships.

History of Science The Chinese used lodestones thousands of years ago. They discovered that if a lodestone swings freely, one end points north. A Chinese general used this method to lead his army through heavy fog.

In about 1600, an English doctor named William Gilbert made a compass needle that acted the same toward the earth as it did toward a lodestone. This showed that the earth itself is a magnet. Now scientists know that the earth, like all magnets, has a south magnetic pole, a north magnetic pole, and a magnetic field.

Notice the compass in the picture. A **compass** is a small magnet that can turn freely. Its north-seeking pole points toward north. Today people use a compass to find directions.

The earth's north magnetic pole is about 1,600 kilometers from its north geographic pole. The compass is pointing toward the north magnetic pole. ▼

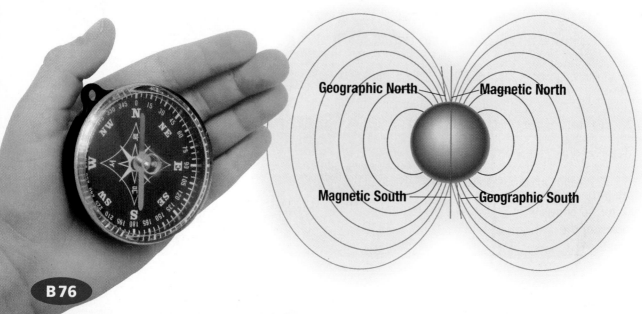

Geographic North   Magnetic North

Magnetic South   Geographic South

Earth Science

If you live in the far northern parts of the United States or Canada, you can sometimes see the northern lights. The lights, as shown in the picture, are caused by the earth's magnetic field. You remember how bits of iron are pulled and pushed into a pattern around a magnet's poles. Charged particles from the sun are pulled and pushed into patterns in the sky near the earth's magnetic poles. The particles react with gases in the air, making the brightly colored lights.

▲ *The northern lights, seen near the earth's magnetic north pole, are also called the* aurora borealis. *Lights seen near the earth's magnetic south pole are called the southern lights, or* aurora australis.

Lesson 3 Review

1. What is magnetism?

2. How is the earth's magnetism useful?

3. **Cause and Effect**
   What causes the northern and southern lights to occur?

Making an Electromagnet

Process Skills

- observing
- making operational definitions

Materials

- safety goggles
- metric ruler
- insulated wire with ends stripped
- bolt
- paper clip
- directional compass
- D-cell battery
- battery holder

Getting Ready

You can find out how electricity is related to magnetism by making an electromagnet. You will learn more about electromagnets in the next lesson.

Look at the self-assessment section at the end of the activity. This tells you what your teacher will expect of you.

Follow This Procedure

1 Make a chart like the one shown. Use your chart to record your observations.

	Bolt held near	
	Paper clip	**Compass**
Circuit disconnected		
Circuit connected		

2 Put on your safety goggles. Measure about 25 cm from one end of the wire. Start near the head of the bolt. Wind the wire tightly around the bolt 20 times (Photo A).

3 Hold the head of the bolt near a paper clip. Record your observations.

4 Hold the head of the bolt near the needle of a compass. Record your observations.

Photo A

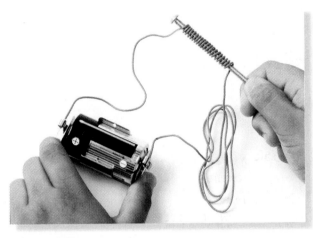

Photo B

5 Place the battery in the battery holder. Attach the ends of the wire to the clips on the battery holder (Photo B). Electricity is now flowing.

 Safety Note If the bolt and battery begin to feel warm, disconnect the battery and allow them to cool.

6 Repeat steps 3 and 4. Record your observations. Disconnect the circuit.

Self-Monitoring
Have I correctly completed all the steps?

Interpret Your Results

1. Write an **operational definition** of an electromagnet. Remember: An operational definition describes what the object does, or what you can observe about the object.

2. Write the definition of an electromagnet found on page B82.

3. How are the two definitions alike? How are they different?

? Inquire Further

What other objects can be attracted by an electromagnet? Develop a plan to answer this or other questions you may have.

Self-Assessment

- I followed instructions to make an electromagnet.
- I **observed** the effects of the electromagnet when no electric current was flowing.
- I observed the effects of the electromagnet when electric current was flowing.
- I recorded my observations.
- I wrote an **operational definition** of an electromagnet, and I compared and contrasted it with the textbook definition.

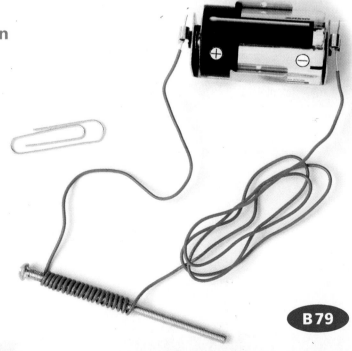

You will learn:

- how a magnet can make electricity.
- how electricity can make a magnet.
- how electromagnets are useful.

Lesson 4

How Do Electricity and Magnetism Work Together?

Brrring! A telephone rings. **Beeeeep!** An alarm clock beeps. **Ding-Dong!** A doorbell chimes. All of these things work because electricity and magnetism work together.

Electricity from Magnets

Magnets and electricity are closely linked. You already know that they act in some similar ways. However, you may not know that you can make electricity using magnets. The electric current that lights the lamp in the picture is made from a magnet.

Find the magnets in the pictures on the next page. Wires are wound in loops or coils around the magnets. The wires are attached to meters that measure electric current.

◀ The electricity used to light lamps in your home is made by powerful magnets in a power plant.

▲ When no electric current flows, the pointer points straight up, at 0.

▲ The pointer moves or jumps when electric current flows. As a student moves the magnet back and forth inside the wire coil, the pointer moves. Electricity is flowing through the wire.

The picture shows how electric current can be made, or generated, by moving a magnet through coils of wire. Electricity can be made from a magnet in several ways. You can slide a magnet back and forth inside a coiled wire or spin a magnet inside a coiled wire. You might also slide a coiled wire back and forth along a magnet or spin a coiled wire around a magnet.

The coiled wire and magnet make just a small model, but it shows how electricity is generated for your home. Most electric power is made by large machines called **generators.** Generators have huge magnets and huge coils of wire. Of course, they are too heavy to move or turn by hand. Some electric generators are powered by wind or rushing water. Others are powered by steam produced by nuclear power or by the burning of coal, gas, or oil.

Glossary

generator
(jen′ə rā′tər), a machine that uses an energy source and a magnet to make electricity

Glossary

Glossary

Glossary

electromagnet
(i lek′trō mag′nit), a magnet made when an electric current flows through a wire

Magnets from Electricity

History of Science

About 180 years ago, a scientist named Hans Christian Oersted was experimenting with electricity. Oersted connected some wire to a large battery so that electricity would flow through the wire. To his surprise, he noticed that when the electric current flowed through the wire something else happened. The needle on a nearby compass moved and pointed toward the wire. Oersted then realized that electricity and magnetism are linked. He concluded that electric current causes a wire to become magnetic.

An **electromagnet** is a temporary magnet made when electric current flows through a wire coil. The picture on this page shows one way to make an electromagnet. If you pass electricity through a coiled wire, the wire becomes magnetic. When the electric current stops flowing, the wire loses its magnetism.

Electric current makes any wire magnetic. Notice the direction that each compass needle is pointing. ▶

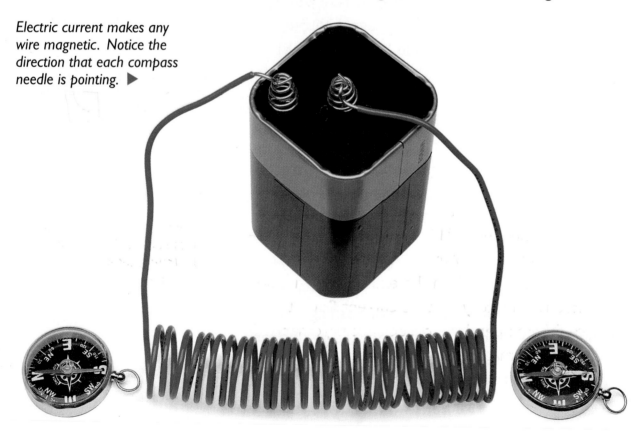

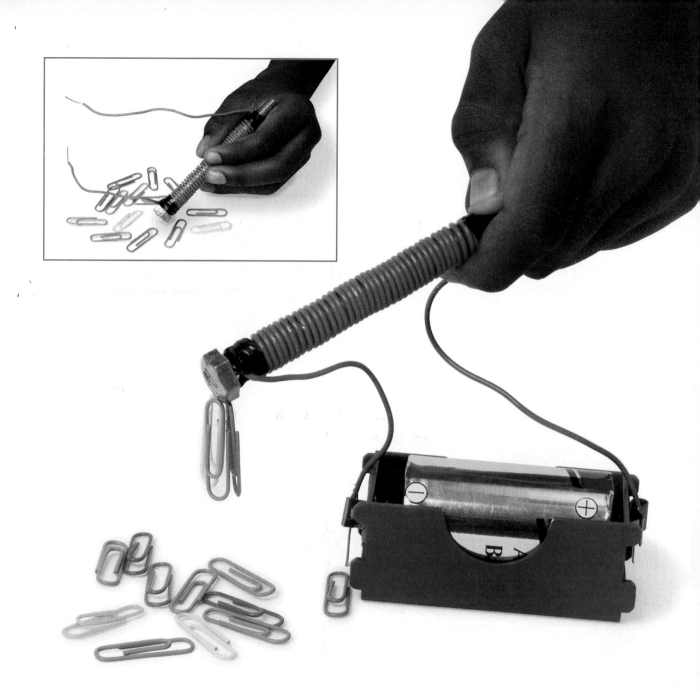

Now look at the picture above showing a wire wrapped around a bolt. This is another way to make an electromagnet. The wire is wrapped about 40 times around a bolt. When the ends of the wire are connected to a battery, electric current flows through the wire. The bolt and the coiled wire together make an electromagnet that is stronger than the electromagnet made with the coiled wire alone.

▲ *The magnetic field of the wire joins the magnetic field of the bolt. This makes an electromagnet strong enough to pick up paper clips.*

Many Uses for Electromagnets

Electromagnets have many uses because they can be turned on and off by closing and opening an electric circuit. The appliances shown on this page all have electromagnets that make them work.

▲ *The pushing of the doorbell closes an electric circuit. Then electric current flows through an electromagnet, and the doorbell rings.*

▲ *When the switch on a fan is turned on, electric current creates an electromagnet that runs the motor in the fan.*

▲ *When electricity flows through an electromagnet in a telephone, the telephone rings.*

Lesson 4 Review

1. How can a coil of wire and a magnet be used to make electricity?

2. How can electricity be used to make a magnet?

3. Why are electromagnets sometimes more useful than ordinary magnets?

4. **Cause and Effect**
   In your own words, write in the correct order the steps that describe how an electric fan runs.

Experimenting with Electromagnets

Materials

- safety goggles
- 25 large paper clips
- metric ruler
- insulated wire with ends stripped
- bolt
- D-cell battery
- battery holder

Process Skills

- formulating questions and hypotheses
- identifying and controlling variables
- experimenting
- estimating and measuring
- collecting and interpreting data
- communicating

Process Skills

State the Problem

How does the number of coils in an electromagnet affect its strength?

Formulate Your Hypothesis

If you increase the number of coils in an electromagnet, will its strength increase, decrease, or remain the same? Write your **hypothesis.**

Identify and Control the Variables

The number of coils is the **variable** you can change. You will perform three trials. Use 20 coils of wire in Trial 1 and 30 coils of wire in Trial 2. You may choose the number of coils for Trial 3. Use the same bolt, wire, and battery for each trial.

Test Your Hypothesis

Follow these steps to perform an **experiment.**

❶ Make a chart like the one on the next page. Use your chart to record your data.

❷ Put on your safety goggles. Bend a paper clip to form a hook (Photo A).

Continued ➜

Photo A

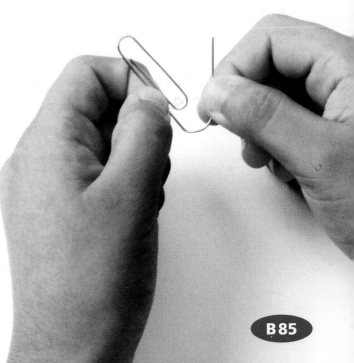

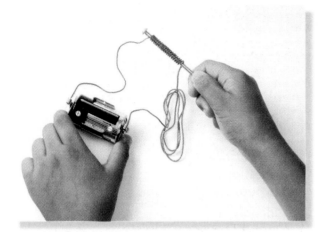

Photo B

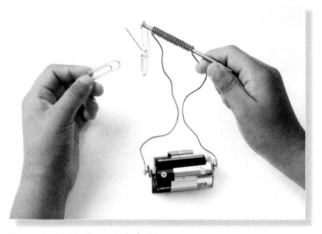

Photo C

3 Construct an electromagnet as you did in the activity on page B78. Place the battery in the battery holder.

4 Attach the ends of the wire to the clips on the battery holder. Electricity is now flowing in the wire (Photo B).

 Safety Note *If the bolt and battery begin to feel warm, disconnect the battery and allow them to cool.*

5 Now you will **measure** the strength of the electromagnet. Pick up the hook-shaped clip with the head of the electromagnet (Photo C). Place paper clips, one at a time, on the hook until the hook falls off. Record the number of paper clips the electromagnet held. Be sure to count the hook-shaped clip. **Collect** and record your **data** in your chart.

6 Disconnect the battery and change the number of coils around the bolt for Trial 2. Repeat steps 4 and 5.

7 Disconnect the battery, and change the number of coils around the bolt for Trial 3. Repeat steps 4 and 5. Then disconnect the battery.

Collect Your Data

Trial	Coils of wire on the electromagnet	Number of clips held
1	20	
2	30	
3		

Interpret Your Data

1. Label a piece of grid paper as shown. Use the data from your chart to make a bar graph on your grid paper.

2. Study your graph. Describe what happened to the number of paper clips held as the number of coils increased or decreased.

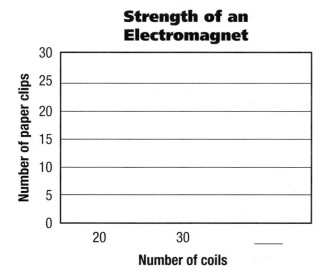

Strength of an Electromagnet

Number of paper clips: 0, 5, 10, 15, 20, 25, 30

Number of coils: 20, 30, _____

State Your Conclusion

How do your results compare with your hypothesis? Explain how the number of coils affects the strength of an electromagnet. **Communicate.** Discuss your conclusion with the class.

Inquire Further

If you add another battery to the electromagnet, will its strength increase? Develop a plan to answer this or other questions you may have.

Self-Assessment

- I made a **hypothesis** about the strength of an electromagnet.
- I **identified** and **controlled variables.**
- I followed instructions to perform an **experiment** with an electromagnet.
- I **collected** and **interpreted** data by recording **measurements** and making a graph.
- I **communicated** by stating my conclusion about the number of coils and strength of an electromagnet.

Chapter 3 Review

Chapter Main Ideas

Lesson 1
• An object gets an electric charge when it gains or loses negative charges.
• An electric current will not flow unless it has a closed pathway, or circuit, to flow through.

Lesson 2
• Series circuits and parallel circuits are two types of electric circuits.
• You need to use electricity safely because it can be dangerous.

Lesson 3
• Magnets have a magnetic field that is strongest at its poles.
• A compass works because of the earth's magnetism.

Lesson 4
• A magnet moving inside a coil of wire makes electricity.
• An electric current flowing through a wire causes the wire to become magnetic.
• Electromagnets are useful in the home because they can be turned on and off.

Reviewing Science Words and Concepts

Write the letter of the word or phrase that best completes each sentence.

a. compass
b. conductor
c. electromagnet
d. generator
e. insulator
f. magnet
g. magnetic field
h. magnetism
i. parallel circuit
j. poles
k. resistance
l. series circuit

1. An electric current passes easily through a wire that is a ___.

2. A material's ___ measures how much the material opposes the flow of electric current.

3. A circuit that connects several objects in a single path is a ___.

4. An object that attracts iron and steel is a ___.

5. An electric current does not pass easily through an ___.

6. The force around a magnet is ___.

7. When electric current runs through a loop of wire, it makes an ___.

8. A small magnet that can turn freely is a ___.

9. The current for each appliance has its own path in a ___.

10. A machine that uses an energy source and a magnet to make electricity is a ___.

11. The space around a magnet where magnetism acts is a ___.

12. Magnetism is strongest at the ___ of a magnet.

Explaining Science

Draw and label a diagram or write a paragraph to answer these questions:

1. How does an object get a positive or negative charge?

2. How are a series circuit and a parallel circuit different?

3. Where is the magnetic field around a magnet strongest?

4. How does an electromagnet work?

Using Skills

1. Use **cause** and **effect** to explain how an electromagnet is useful.

2. How does the use of electricity make your life different than it would be without electricity? **Communicate** your thoughts by writing a paragraph.

3. Suppose you saw a bunch of balloons tied together, but none of the balloons were touching one another. What might you **infer** about the electric charges on the balloons?

Critical Thinking

1. You construct a circuit, but electricity will not flow through it. **Draw a conclusion** about what kind of circuit you think you constructed. Explain your reasoning.

2. Imagine you have just combed your hair with a plastic comb. You hold the comb near a small stream of water running from a faucet. You are amazed that the water stream bends toward the comb. What would you **infer** caused the stream of water to be attracted to the comb?

3. A friend is going to wire a model house. He is not sure if he should wire the lights in a series or parallel circuit. **Make a decision** about the best kind of circuit to use. Write him a note telling him what you think he should do and why it would be best.

Turn on the Music!

Did you know that without light you could not play your CDs? The great music you hear from your CDs is the result of reflected light!

Chapter 4
Light and Sound

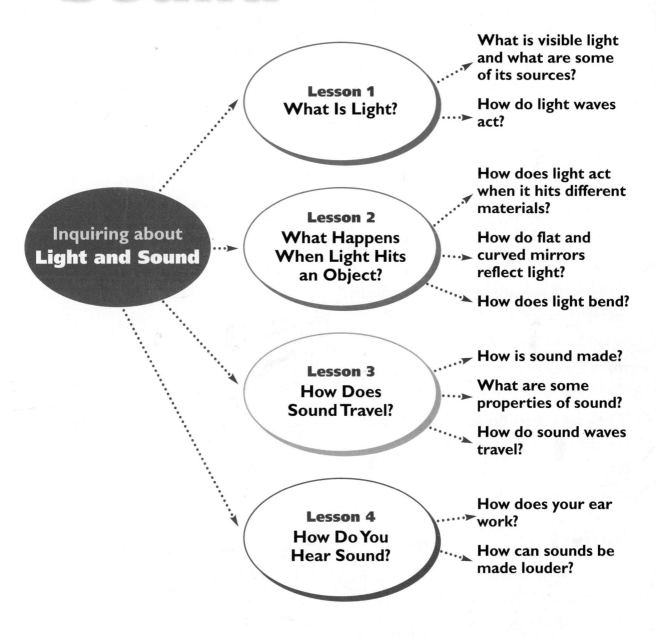

Inquiring about Light and Sound

Lesson 1
What Is Light?

What is visible light and what are some of its sources?

How do light waves act?

Lesson 2
What Happens When Light Hits an Object?

How does light act when it hits different materials?

How do flat and curved mirrors reflect light?

How does light bend?

Lesson 3
How Does Sound Travel?

How is sound made?

What are some properties of sound?

How do sound waves travel?

Lesson 4
How Do You Hear Sound?

How does your ear work?

How can sounds be made louder?

Copy the chapter graphic organizer onto your own paper. This organizer shows you what the whole chapter is all about. As you read the lessons and do the activities, look for answers to the questions and write them on your organizer.

Exploring Colors in Light

Process Skills

- observing
- communicating

Materials

- direct sunlight
- white sheet of paper
- prism
- colored pencils

Explore

1 Hold a piece of white paper so the sunlight shines on it. The sun should be behind you. What color does the sunlight appear to be on the paper?

2 Hold the prism so that the sunlight shines through it. Move the prism around until the sunlight strikes the white piece of paper. You should move the prism until you see different colors.

3 What colors do you see? What is the order of the colors you see? Record your **observations.** Make a drawing of the colors.

Reflect

1. When the sunlight passes through a prism, colors that are in sunlight become visible. Describe how the prism changed the appearance of the sunlight.

2. Where have you seen colors like this before? **Communicate.** Discuss your observations with the class. Compare and contrast your observations and your drawing with others in the class.

Inquire Further

What happens if you shine light from a lamp through the prism? Develop a plan to answer this or other questions you may have.

Using Graphic Sources

In the Explore Activity, *Exploring Colors in Light*, you studied some of the properties of light. The drawing you made in the activity helped you to understand that sunlight is made up of all the colors of the rainbow and the colors in between. Drawings and photographs are examples of graphic sources. Tables, charts, and diagrams are some other examples. Because **graphic sources** show information visually, they can help make facts and ideas clearer.

Example

In Lesson 1, *What Is Light?*, you discover that light is a form of energy. You also learn that different colors of light have different wavelengths. The diagram below provides information about a rainbow. The parts of the diagram include a drawing, labels, and a caption. Use the diagram to answer the questions below.

Colors of Light in a Rainbow						
Violet	Indigo	Blue	Green	Yellow	Orange	Red

Short wavelength   Long wavelength

▲ *Each color of light in a rainbow has a different wavelength.*

Reading Vocabulary

graphic source (graf′ik sôrs), drawing, photograph, table, chart, or diagram that shows information visually

▲ *Have you ever wondered what causes a rainbow?*

Talk About It!

1. What are the colors of the rainbow?

2. Which color has the longest wavelength? the shortest?

What's the Big Idea?

You will learn:

- what visible light is and what some of its sources are.
- how light waves act.

Lesson 1

What Is Light?

WOW! That may be what you thought when you last saw a rainbow. Was it in the sky after a rainstorm? Or was the rainbow made by the sun shining through water? What causes a rainbow to appear?

Visible Light and Its Sources

Can you imagine what the world would be like without light? You would not be able to see the world around you. Plants could not grow, and you would not have any food to eat.

Light is all around you, but you probably don't think about it very often. Do you know that light is really energy? Unlike most energy, light is a form of energy that you can see. The light energy that you can see is the **visible spectrum.**

Notice the rainbow in the picture. You might have seen a rainbow in the sky after a rain shower. When the sun shines through the clouds during or after a rain shower, the sunlight passes through water droplets in the air. The droplets break up the light into all the colors of the visible spectrum, making a rainbow.

◀ *Water droplets in the air act like prisms and break white light into the colors of the visible spectrum.*

Look at the rainbow again. You can see the colors—red, orange, yellow, green, blue, indigo, and violet—in the rainbow. All of these colors, and the colors in between them, make up white light. Light from the sun is white light.

Most of our light comes from the sun. Even moonlight is light from the sun bouncing off the moon. However, some other objects are sources of light. Which objects in the pictures give off light? The sun, fire, and electric lights are all sources of light. Candles, matches, and flashlights also make light.

The burning wood, the electric lights, and the sun all produce light. ▶

Glossary

wavelength
(wāv′lengkth′), the distance from a point on a wave to the same point on the next wave

How Light Waves Act

You may have used a flashlight to see in a dark place. If so, you know that the flashlight shines brightly on an object nearby. If you shine the flashlight on an object farther away, the light isn't as bright because it spreads out.

Light energy moves in a straight line away from its source in waves. If you have thrown a stone into water, you have seen how waves move out away from the stone. Light waves move somewhat like waves in water. Unlike the waves in water, light waves can move through empty space.

The picture shows a light wave that might come from the flashlight. The distance from a point on a wave to the same point on the next wave is the light's **wavelength**. Different colors of light have different wavelengths. Other kinds of energy also have waves like light waves. Microwaves, X rays, and radio waves are like light waves. However, they have wavelengths that are different from light wavelengths, and you can't see them.

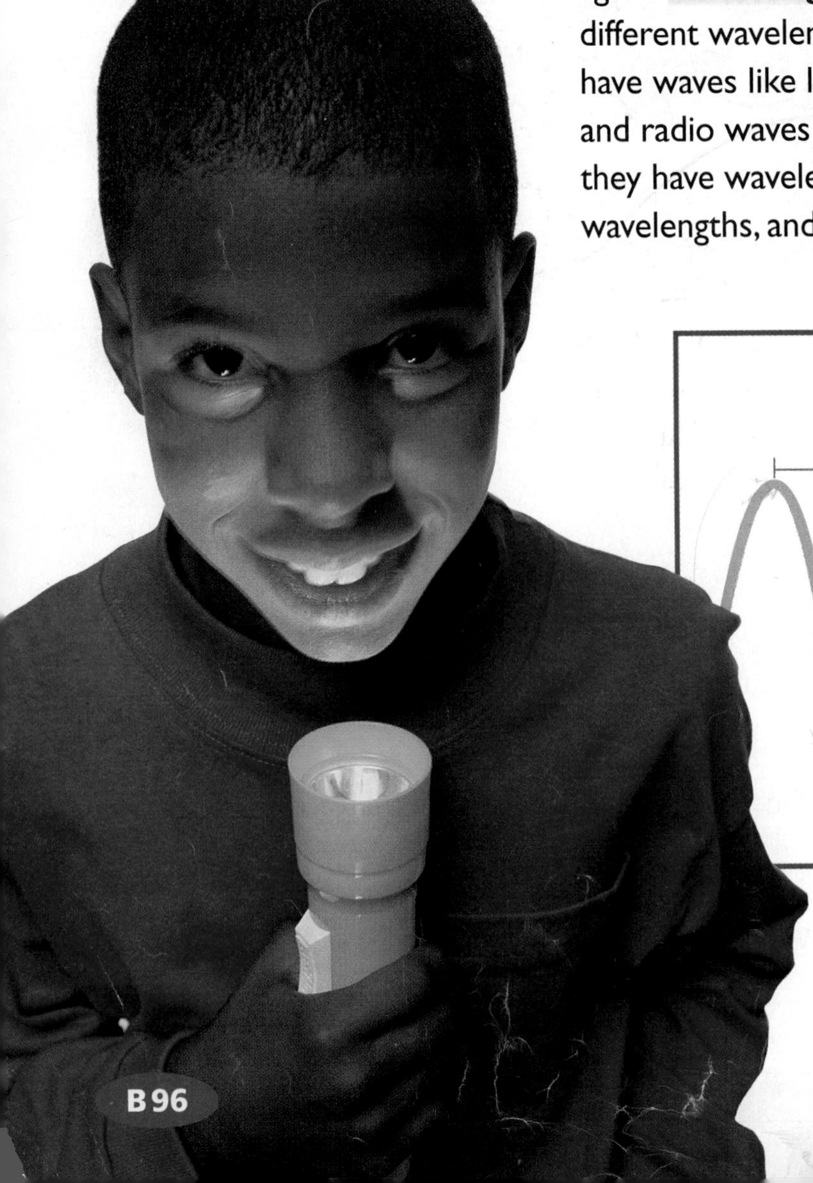

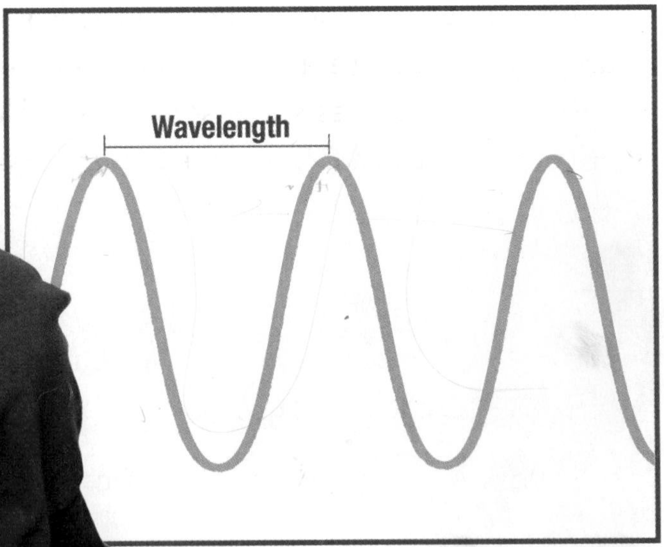

Wavelength

◀ Light from the flashlight moves in a straight line away from the flashlight in waves.

B 96

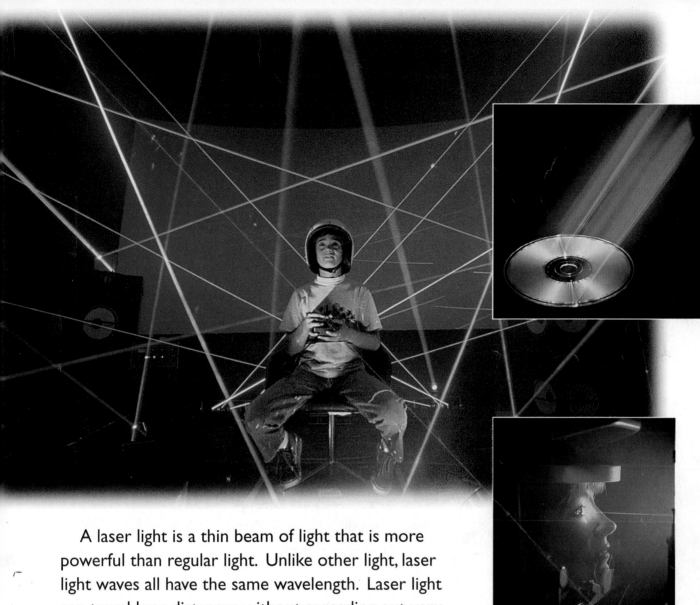

A laser light is a thin beam of light that is more powerful than regular light. Unlike other light, laser light waves all have the same wavelength. Laser light can travel long distances without spreading out very much and is therefore useful in communications and medicine. The pictures show some uses of laser light—a light show, a CD scanner, and eye surgery.

▲ Laser light beams can be fun, as well as useful.

Lesson 1 Review

1. What is light, and where does it come from?
2. How are light waves different from waves in water?
3. **Graphic Sources**
   Describe what happens to the light as it moves away from the flashlight on page B96.

What's the Big Idea?

You will learn:
- how light acts when it hits different materials.
- how flat and curved mirrors reflect light.
- how light bends.

Glossary

transparent
(tran spâr′ənt), allows light to pass through so that whatever is behind can be seen

translucent
(tran slü′snt), allows light to pass through but scatters it so that whatever is behind it cannot be clearly seen

Lesson 2

What Happens When Light Hits an Object?

Have you ever watched sunlight shining through a stained glass window? If the sunlight hits a wall, you can see the beautiful colors. **AMAZING!** Why do you think this happens?

Different Materials and Light

Notice the pictures below. In the first picture, you can see the picture behind the glass. You can see the picture because glass is **transparent.** Light passes through a transparent object, and you can see what is behind it. Clear glass, clean water, and clear plastic are transparent.

Now look at the second picture. You can see the picture, but it is not as clear as in the first picture. Light passes through the thin paper, but the paper spreads the light around in different directions. The thin paper is **translucent.** Tissue paper, wax paper, and some kinds of glass and plastic are translucent.

▲ Transparent

▲ Translucent

▲ Opaque

In the third picture, you cannot see the picture behind the paper at all. Light cannot pass through the paper covering the picture. The paper is **opaque.** You cannot see through opaque material. Bricks, wood, and your book are opaque.

Have you ever wondered why you can see colors? You see colors because of what happens to light when it hits different materials. You also see colors because white light is made up of all the colors. Look at the pictures below and read to find out what happens.

Glossary

opaque (ō pāk′), does not allow light to pass through

transmit (tran smit′), to allow to pass through

absorb (ab sôrb′), to take in

reflect (ri flekt′), to bounce back

Seeing Color of Transparent and Translucent Objects

◀ The blue glass looks blue because it absorbs all the colors in light except blue. Blue glass lets blue light pass through it. Therefore, it looks blue. Transparent and translucent objects are the color of the light they **transmit,** or let pass through.

Seeing Color of Opaque Objects

When light hits the chili pepper in the picture, the pepper **absorbs,** or takes in, all the colors in the light except red. The pepper looks red because it **reflects,** or bounces back, the red light. Then why do some objects look white? That's right! A white object reflects all the colors in white light. However, black objects absorb almost all of the light that hits them. They do not reflect any colors of light. ▼

Mirrors and Light

When you look at some objects, you see your image. When you look at other objects, you do not see your image. Why does this happen?

To answer this question, first you must think about how you see objects. You know that if you are in a totally dark room, you cannot see anything. You see objects because the objects reflect light to your eyes.

If you place objects in front of a flat mirror, you see an image of the objects. The flat mirror in the picture, like all mirrors, has a smooth, shiny surface. Notice that the light rays hit the mirror at a certain angle or direction. Also notice that the rays reflect off the mirror at the same angle or direction. You can see a good image of the toys.

In the other picture, the toys are in front of a rough wall. Notice that when light rays hit the rough surface, they reflect in many different directions. You cannot see an image of the toys.

The picture shows how light rays reflect off the flat mirror. ▼

The picture shows how light rays reflect off the rough surface. ▼

◀ *The picture shows how light waves reflect off the curved mirror in a fun house.*

Notice the picture of the fun house mirror. Why do you think the image looks so strange? Each light ray that hits the surface of the curved mirror is reflected back at the same angle that it hits. Because the surface is curved, the light rays that hit the mirror in different places bounce off in different directions. Therefore, you do not see a good image. The image may be larger or smaller—or even upside down.

Curved mirrors can be fun, but they can also be useful. Curved mirrors are used in stores so that clerks can see people all over the stores. The mirrors in some cars are curved to help drivers see a larger area of traffic behind them.

How Light Bends

Why do you think the stems of the flowers in the picture seem to be broken? The stems look broken because light sometimes bends or changes direction.

Have you ever tried to run through sand or deep snow? If so, you know that you can't run as fast as on solid ground. Light also travels at different speeds through different materials. However, when light changes speed, it also changes direction. Light bends when it moves from one material to another.

The light rays that reflect from the top of the flowers in the vase move through air. These rays do not bend. The light rays that reflect from the stems in the water travel back through the water before they reach the air. Light travels faster through air than it does through water. When these rays move into the air, they change speed and bend. The stems look broken.

Notice the lenses in the pictures on the next page. A lens is a transparent object that has at least one curved surface. When light moves from air into a lens, the light bends. Lenses bend light in a way that makes an image.

◀ *When light bends, it makes objects look different than they really are.*

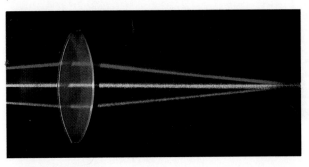

▲ Convex lens

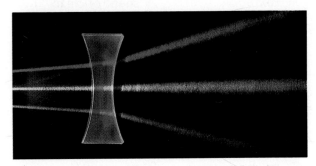

▲ Concave lens

The lens in the first picture bulges in the middle like a football. This kind of lens is a **convex lens.** Notice how the convex lens bends light. Each of your eyes has a convex lens. The microscope in the picture also uses convex lenses.

The lens in the second picture is thinner in the middle than at the edges. This kind of lens is a **concave lens.** Notice that the concave lens spreads light rays apart. A concave lens makes objects look smaller.

Lesson 2 Review

1. Why do some objects look white?

2. How does a curved mirror help a car driver?

3. What happens to light rays when they move from water into air?

4. **Graphic Sources**
   Use the pictures above to help you describe what happens to light rays as they pass through lenses.

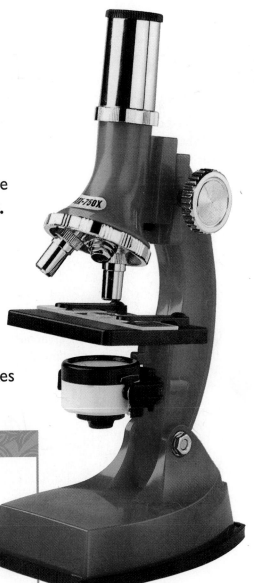

▲ Convex lenses in a microscope make small objects look much larger.

Observing Light Through Different Materials

Process Skills

- observing
- inferring

Materials

- textbook
- small object to cast shadow
- sheet of white construction paper
- flashlight
- sheet of clear plastic
- sheet of wax paper
- sheet of aluminum foil

Getting Ready

In this activity you will observe how different materials transmit light.

Follow This Procedure

❶ Make a chart like the one shown. Use your chart to record your observations.

Material held in front of flashlight	Observations of shadow of object
No material	
Clear plastic	
Wax paper	
Aluminum foil	

❷ Darken the room. Place the textbook on a desk. Place the object on the textbook. Have a partner hold the sheet of white construction paper behind the textbook and object.

❸ Shine a flashlight on the object so that a shadow appears on the construction paper (Photo A). How does the shadow appear? Are the edges of the shadow clear and sharp? Record your **observations.**

❹ Continue shining the flashlight on the object while holding a sheet of clear plastic in front of the flashlight (Photo B). Look at the shadow of the object. Record your observations.

❺ Repeat step 4 using wax paper.

❻ Repeat step 4 using aluminum foil.

Photo A

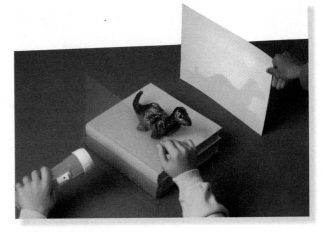

Photo B

Self-Monitoring

Did I notice differences in steps 4, 5, and 6? Do I need to repeat any of my observations to make sure?

Interpret Your Results

1. Compare and contrast the shadows you observed. Which material formed the sharpest shadow? Which material formed a shadow that was not sharp?

2. Describe what you observed when the aluminum foil was placed in front of the flashlight. Make an **inference.** Which material transmits the most light? Which material transmits the least light?

Inquire Further

What do you think will happen to the shadow of the object if you move the object closer to or farther away from the white construction paper? Develop a plan to answer this or other questions you may have.

Self-Assessment

- I followed instructions to investigate how different materials transmit light.
- I **observed** what happened to the shadows when different materials were placed between the flashlight and the object.
- I recorded my observations.
- I compared and contrasted the shadows produced.
- I made an **inference** about the light transmitted through the different materials.

You will learn:

- how sound is made.
- what some properties of sound are.
- how sound waves travel.

Glossary

vibrate (vī′brāt), to move quickly back and forth

Lesson 3

How Does Sound Travel?

SCREECH! Sounds are all around you. Stop and listen a minute. What sounds do you hear? You might hear doors closing, people talking, or dogs barking. What makes these sounds?

How Sound Is Made

You know that light is a kind of energy that you can see. Sound is also a kind of energy, but you can't see sound. However, you can hear sound. Sometimes you might even feel sound.

Each of the instruments that the children in the picture are playing makes a different sound. The sound of music is different from a door banging or the crack of a bat against a baseball. However, all of these sounds are alike in some ways.

The sounds of doors, bats, and music are made in the same way. All these sounds are made when matter **vibrates,** or moves quickly back and forth.

Anything that takes up space is matter. Even though you cannot see it, air is matter. The instruments in the picture, the air, and the children are all made of matter.

If you pluck the strings of a guitar, you make the strings vibrate. Each string makes a different sound, and you make music. If you hit a drum, you make the drum vibrate. Then the drum makes a booming sound. Even though these sounds are very different, each of the sounds is made when something makes matter vibrate.

The children cause each of the instruments to vibrate, and music is made. ▼

Properties of Sound

Now you know how the drum makes sound, but how can you hear the sound? The booming of the drum must reach your ear. When the drum begins to vibrate, sound waves move out from the drum. As the sound waves move through the air, they make the air vibrate. Look at the picture on the left and read to find out more about sound waves.

◀ Sound Waves
Sound waves are different from light waves. Sound waves are more like the waves that move through the spring shown here. Notice that in some places the parts of the spring are close together. When sound vibrations move through matter, they push the particles of matter closer together. As the sound vibrations pass, the particles move apart again.

Wavelength
The wavelength of a sound wave is the distance from a point on one part of a wave to the same point on the next wave.

The boy uses a lot of energy to shout and makes a loud sound. A person can hear him at a long distance. ▼

You have seen how sounds are alike. Now look at some ways that sounds are different. Notice the picture on page B108 of the boy shouting. A shout is a loud sound. It has more **volume** than a whisper. The girls in the picture on this page are whispering. A whisper is a soft sound. Now look at the graph. Find another soft sound on the graph.

What makes some sounds louder than others? You know that when you shout you put a lot of energy into it. You use much less energy to whisper. Also, if you have ever hit a drum, you know that you can make the drum sound loud or soft. If you hit the drum lightly, the drum makes a soft sound. If you hit the drum hard, the drum makes a loud sound. It takes more energy for you to hit the drum hard, so the sound waves have more energy, and the sound is louder.

A lion's roar or the sound of an airplane's engine are some other loud sounds. A bird singing and a gentle breeze blowing through leaves make soft sounds. What other loud sounds and soft sounds can you think of?

Volume of Sound

People whispering

Bird singing

Jet landing

Soft ⟶ Loud

◀ The girl uses only a little energy to whisper. To hear a whisper, a person must be nearby.

Glossary

pitch (pich), the highness or lowness of a sound

Sounds can also be different in other ways. If you have ever heard the music from a trombone, you know that it sounds very low. What makes a trombone sound so low? Notice how large the trombone in the picture is. When the child blows air into the large trombone, the air vibrates slowly. Because the air vibrates slowly, the sound waves from the trombone are very long. Sound waves that have long wavelengths make a sound with a low pitch. The **pitch** of a sound is how high or how low the sound is.

Look at the flute in the picture. Would you expect the flute to play a sound with a low pitch or a high pitch? If you said "high," you're right. The flute has a smaller opening through it than a trombone does. When the child blows air into the flute, the air vibrates quickly. The sound waves have short wavelengths, and the sound has a high pitch.

The larger column of air in the trombone does not vibrate as quickly as the smaller column of air in the flute. ▼

Think about the strings on a guitar. Some of the strings are thin and some of the strings are thick. If you pluck the thin strings of the guitar, they vibrate quickly. The thin strings make sounds with a high pitch. If you pluck the thick strings, they vibrate slowly. The thick strings make sounds with a low pitch.

You probably enjoy listening to music. What kinds of music do you like? Your family or friends may not like the same music that you do. Rock music may sound pleasant to you, but some friends may think that rock is too noisy. However, most people enjoy listening to some kind of music. Music is usually thought to be a pleasant sound.

The world around you is filled with sounds. Some of the sounds are pleasant, but some of the sounds are not so pleasant. Sounds made by the leaves in the picture below are pleasant sounds. Birds singing or a gentle rainfall are also pleasant sounds.

Other sounds, such as a jet plane taking off, are unpleasant sounds, or noise. Brakes screeching and car horns blowing are also noisy sounds. Too much noise can be harmful to your health. Notice that the airport worker in the picture above is wearing ear protectors. They keep the noise from harming her ears.

Beside being harmful to your ears, noise can affect you in other ways. Being in a noisy place for a long time can make people feel upset. Noise can also affect the way people sleep or digest food.

Even listening to pleasant sounds, such as music, can be harmful. Listening to loud music or other loud sounds for long periods of time can cause hearing loss. If you use earphones to listen to music, be sure to keep the volume low.

▲ This airport worker is wearing ear protectors. Without them, she could suffer hearing loss because of the loud noises.

When leaves fall, they make a very soft sound. ▼

How Sound Travels Through Different Materials

As you know, sound waves, unlike light waves, cannot travel through empty space. Since sound waves travel by making matter vibrate, they must travel through matter. However, sound waves travel faster in some materials than they do in other materials. Look at the pictures and read to find out why this happens.

◀ How Sound Travels Through Air
When the bird in the picture chirps, the sound waves make the particles in the air vibrate. When the particles vibrate, they bump into other particles. The sound waves move from one particle of air to the next. Notice how far apart the air particles are. The sound waves move slowly from one particle of air to the next.

How Sound Travels Through Water
When the whale in the picture sings, the sound waves make the particles in water vibrate. The sound waves move from one particle of water to the next. Notice that the particles in the water are closer than the particles in the air. The particles of water bump into one another faster than the air particles do. Therefore, sound waves move faster in water than they do in air. ▼

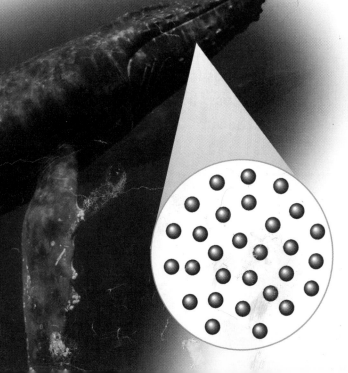

How Sound Travels Through Wood

When the child in the picture taps on the door, the sound waves make the particles in the wood vibrate. Notice how close together the wood particles are. They are almost touching one another. The particles of wood bump into one another very quickly. The sound waves move quickly from one particle of wood to the next. Sound waves travel faster in a material such as wood than they do in air or water. ▶

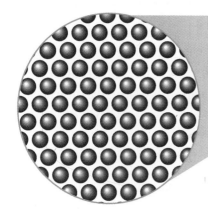

Lesson 3 Review

1. How does hitting a drum cause the drum to make a sound?

2. When does an object make sound with a high pitch?

3. Why does sound travel faster through wood than it does through water?

4. **Graphic Sources**
   How does the picture of the particles in wood above help to explain why sound travels faster through wood than other materials?

Classifying Sounds

Process Skills

- observing
- classifying
- collecting and interpreting data
- inferring

Materials

- small paper clip
- metric ruler
- large paper clip
- small coin
- large coin
- small rubber band
- large rubber band
- small plastic cup
- large plastic cup
- small ball of aluminum foil
- large ball of aluminum foil

Getting Ready

In this activity you will compare the pitch and volume of sounds.

You will have to listen and concentrate carefully to hear differences in the sounds. You may have to repeat some of the tests until you are sure of your answers.

Follow This Procedure

1 Make a chart like the one shown. Use your chart to record your observations.

2 Drop a paper clip from a height of 10 cm onto a desk (Photo A). **Observe** its pitch.

3 Drop another object from a height of 10 cm. If the pitch is lower than the paper clip, place it on your desk below the clip. If the pitch is higher than that produced by the paper clip, place it on your desk above the paper clip.

Pitch Highest to lowest	Volume Highest to lowest

4 Repeat step 3 with each of the other objects (Photo B). When you are done you will have **classified** the items. They will be placed in order of the pitch they produce, from highest to lowest. **Collect** your **data** by recording the ranked items in your chart.

Photo A

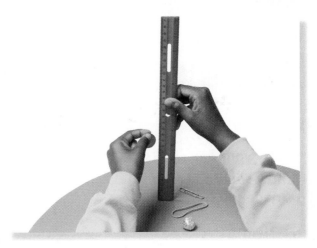

Photo B

⑤ Repeat steps 3 and 4 with all of the objects, but this time rank them by the volume of sound they produce when dropped.

Self-Monitoring
Do I need to repeat any of the steps to be sure of my answers?

Interpret Your Results

1. Interpret your data. Which of the objects made the sound highest in pitch? lowest in pitch? Make an **inference.** What are some properties of objects that produce sounds high in pitch? What are some properties of objects that produce sounds low in pitch?

2. Which of the objects made the sound highest in volume? lowest in volume? Make an inference. What are some properties of objects that produce sounds high in volume? What are some properties of objects that produce sounds low in volume?

Inquire Further

What would happen to the sounds if you dropped the items on different surfaces? Develop a plan to answer this or other questions you may have.

Self-Assessment

- I followed instructions to compare the pitch and volume of sounds produced by different objects.
- I **observed** the sounds produced by dropping different objects.
- I **classified** the sounds of the objects by ranking their pitch and volume.
- I **collected data** by recording the ranking of the objects in a chart.
- I made **inferences** about the properties of objects that produce sounds of different pitch and volume.

You will learn:
- how your ear works.
- how sounds can be made louder.

Lesson 4

How Do You Hear Sound?

Sound plays an important part in your life. **BRRING!** Alarm clocks ring, doorbells ring, school bells ring, and railroad crossing bells ring! How are you able to hear all of these and other sounds?

How Your Ear Works

Human Body

Imagine that you are the child in the picture listening to a CD. You turn on the CD player. How does the music reach your ear so that you can hear it? Sound waves move out from the speakers of the CD player and make the air around them vibrate. The shape of your outer ear directs the sound waves to the part of the ear inside your head. Look at the picture on the next page. Notice how sound waves move through your ear so that you can hear the music.

When the messages get to your brain, it helps you understand the sound that is received. Then you hear the music from the CD player. You know that when you start a CD, you hear the music right away. That's how fast the sound waves travel from the speakers, to your ear, and through your ear to your brain.

Music to sing along with or music to dream by! You can play music for any mood on a CD player. ▼

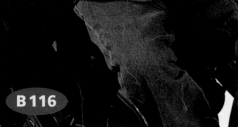

Hearing music is fun, but many of the other sounds you hear help to keep you safe. Hearing some sounds, such as a fire alarm at your school or a smoke alarm in your home, can warn you of danger. Hearing a tornado siren or other storm warning gives you time to move to a safe place.

Life Science Many animals have ears somewhat like your ears. Each of their ears catches sound and directs it to the eardrum. Then the sound waves move through their ears to their brain, and they hear the sound.

However, many animals can hear sounds that you cannot hear. For example, dogs can hear high-pitched sounds that you can't hear. Some animals, such as rabbits, can also hear sounds that are too soft for you to hear. Being able to hear sounds helps keep animals safe.

Three Tiny Bones
As the eardrum vibrates, it causes the three tiny bones to vibrate.

Eardrum
Sound waves hit a thin skin called the eardrum. The sound waves cause the eardrum to vibrate.

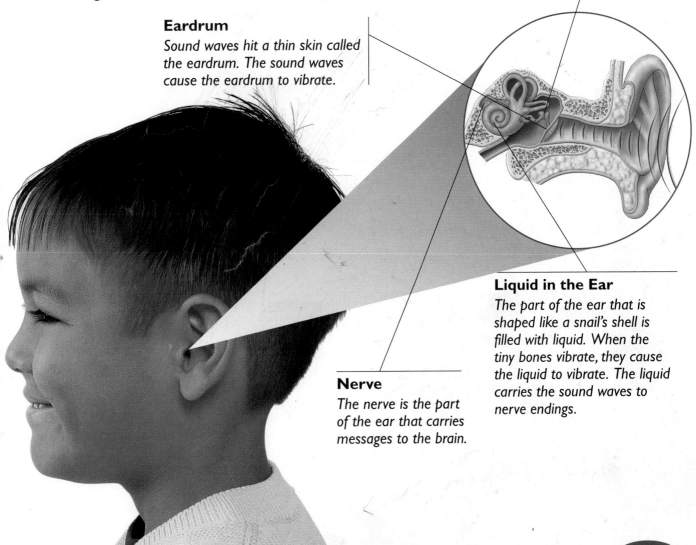

Nerve
The nerve is the part of the ear that carries messages to the brain.

Liquid in the Ear
The part of the ear that is shaped like a snail's shell is filled with liquid. When the tiny bones vibrate, they cause the liquid to vibrate. The liquid carries the sound waves to nerve endings.

Making Sounds Louder

Glossary

stethoscope
(steth′ə skōp), an
instrument used to
hear the sounds of
body organs

microphone
(mī′krə fōn), an
instrument used to
amplify voices, music,
and other sounds

electric signal
(i lek′trik sig′nəl), a
form of energy

amplify (am′plə fī), to
make stronger

bullhorn (bùl′hôrn′),
an instrument with a
built-in microphone that
makes sound louder

Sometimes sounds must be made louder to be heard at a distance. Sounds that warn people of danger must be loud enough to get people's attention. Also, doctors and nurses often must listen to the sound of people's body organs to know if they are healthy. Some of these sounds must be made louder to be heard. Look at the pictures and read the text on pages B118–B121 to find out some ways to make sound louder.

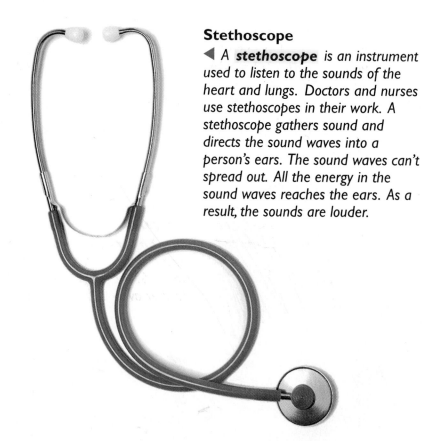

Stethoscope

◀ A **stethoscope** is an instrument used to listen to the sounds of the heart and lungs. Doctors and nurses use stethoscopes in their work. A stethoscope gathers sound and directs the sound waves into a person's ears. The sound waves can't spread out. All the energy in the sound waves reaches the ears. As a result, the sounds are louder.

The doctor in the picture is using a stethoscope to listen to the child's lungs. The lung sounds are louder because the sound waves are directed to his ears by the stethoscope. ▼

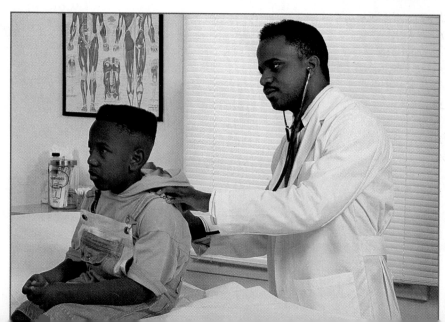

Microphone

A **microphone** can be used to amplify the sound of your voice. The woman in the picture is using a microphone. Sound waves from the woman's voice hit the microphone and make a part inside the microphone vibrate. ▼

The microphone collects the sound waves and changes the sound energy into electric energy, or **electric signals.** The electric energy moves through a wire in the microphone to an amplifier. The amplifier makes the electric energy stronger, or amplifies it. **Amplify** means to make stronger. The stronger electric energy moves to a speaker. The speaker changes the signals back into sound waves. The woman's voice comes out of the speaker with more volume than the sound that entered the microphone. ▶

Bullhorn

◀ A **bullhorn** has a built-in microphone. A bullhorn can increase the energy of the sound waves made by your voice. Sound waves from a bullhorn can be heard much farther away than the unaided voice.

▲ You speak into the mouthpiece of the bullhorn. The microphone changes the sound energy into electric energy. These signals travel to another part of the bullhorn that amplifies them. The amplified signals then move into the speaker of the bullhorn. The speaker changes the signals back into sound waves that have more energy than those that entered the mouthpiece. Having more energy makes the sound louder.

▲ The firefighter in the picture is using a bullhorn to direct people to safety during a fire. The bullhorn allows people who are far away to hear the firefighter.

History of Science

A **hearing aid** is an instrument used to help people with a hearing loss. Hearing aids of different kinds have been used for many years. Look at the pictures and read to find out how hearing aids have changed through the years.

How Hearing Aids Have Changed

One of the early hearing aids was the hearing tube. As you can see, people had to sit close to one another to use this hearing aid. The tube acted somewhat like a stethoscope. It directed the sound of a person's voice to another person's ear. ▶

The first hearing aids with microphones in them were usually large and bulky. They needed electricity to work. The person who wore them had to wear a battery pack. ▶

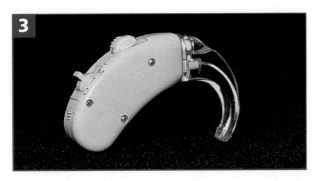

During the 1950s and early 1960s, a tiny battery was made that helped make hearing aids smaller. Some hearing aids were worn behind the ear or on a person's eyeglasses.

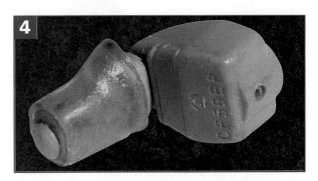

During the 1970s, a hearing aid could fit in a person's outer ear. However, people still had problems with hearing aids. The hearing aid amplified background noises as well as voices. The loud noises made it hard for people to understand voices.

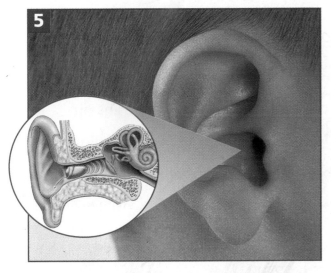

During the late 1970s, a hearing aid was made that could fit entirely in the ear canal.

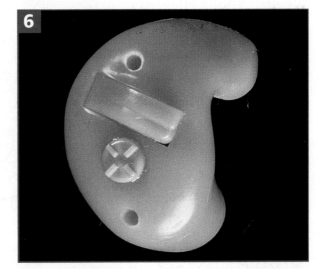

During the 1980s and 1990s, hearing aids have been made with digital controls. A person can program the hearing aid to make hearing better. The batteries in the newer hearing aids also last longer.

Lesson 4 Review

1. Draw a picture to show how sounds travel through the ear.

2. How does a stethoscope make sounds louder?

3. **Graphic Sources**
   Use the pictures and captions on these two pages to make a time line showing the changes in hearing aids.

Chapter 4 Review

Chapter Main Ideas

Lesson 1

• The visible spectrum is light energy that can be seen. The sun, fire, electric lights, candles, matches, and flashlights are all sources of light.

• Light waves move in a straight line away from their source and can move through empty space.

Lesson 2

• Light can be reflected, absorbed, or transmitted when it hits different materials, and the color of light that is reflected or transmitted gives objects their color.

• Flat mirrors reflect good images, while curved mirrors reflect somewhat changed images.

• Lenses cause light rays to bend by changing their speed and direction.

Lesson 3

• Sound is made when matter is caused to vibrate.

• Volume and pitch are properties of sound.

• Sound waves travel through different materials at different speeds; they cannot travel through empty space.

Lesson 4

• You hear sounds when sound waves cause vibrations to move through your ear to a nerve and the nerve then sends messages to the brain.

• Stethoscopes, microphones, bullhorns, and hearing aids can be used to make sounds louder.

Reviewing Words and Concepts

Write the letter of the word or phrase that best completes each sentence.

a. absorb

b. amplify

c. bullhorn

d. concave lens

e. convex lens

f. electric signal

g. hearing aid

h. microphone

i. opaque

j. pitch

k. reflect

l. stethoscope

m. translucent

n. transmit

o. transparent

p. vibrate

q. visible spectrum

r. volume

s. wavelength

1. The _____ is made up of all the colors of the rainbow.

2. People with a hearing loss may use a _____ to help them hear better.

3. The distance from a point on one wave to the same point on the next wave is the _____.

4. A loud sound has more _____ than a soft sound.

5. Light cannot pass through an object that is _____.

6. An opaque object can _____ some colors and reflect others.

7. A _____ is an instrument with a built-in microphone.

8. The color of transparent objects depends on the color they _____.

9. A _____ makes small objects look larger than they are.

10. People may use a _____ to amplify their voices when giving a speech.

11. Wax paper is _____ because it lets light pass through but scatters it.

12. Sound is made when an object is caused to _____.

13. Yellow flowers look yellow because they _____ yellow light.

14. The thin strings on a guitar make sounds with a higher _____ than the sounds made by the thick strings.

15. Doctors and nurses use a _____ to hear the sounds of the heart and lungs.

16. A _____ spreads light rays apart because it is thinner in the middle than at the edges.

17. Microphones change sound waves into an _____.

18. Glass is _____ because you can see through it clearly.

19. If you make a sound stronger, you _____ it.

Explaining Science

Draw and label a picture or write a paragraph to answer these questions.

1. How does light act when it hits different materials?

2. Why do green apples look green?

3. Why do sound waves travel faster in wood than in air?

4. How do you hear a person's voice?

Using Skills

1. How can you use a graphic source to help you understand a difficult concept?

2. Suppose you are in a dark room and you have a white ball. You put the white ball under a red light. Predict what color the ball will appear. Communicate your reason for the prediction by writing a short paragraph.

3. Suppose you observe a rainbow in the sky, but it hasn't rained where you are. What might you infer?

Critical Thinking

1. Classify these sounds as having a high pitch or low pitch: flute, trombone, a singing bird, a roaring lion.

2. Compare and contrast light waves and sound waves.

3. Infer why an opaque object will make a shadow when light hits it.

Unit B Review

Reviewing Words and Concepts

Choose at least three words from the Chapter 1 list below.
Use the words to write a paragraph about how these concepts
are related. Do the same for each of the other chapters.

Chapter 1
density
graduated cylinder
gram
mass
matter
volume

Chapter 2
force
friction
gravity
inertia
kinetic energy
potential energy

Chapter 3
conductor
electromagnet
insulator
magnet
magnetism
resistance

Chapter 4
opaque
pitch
reflect
vibrate
visible spectrum
volume

Reviewing Main Ideas

**Each of the statements below is false. Change the
underlined word or words to make each statement true.**

1. A <u>solution</u> is anything that can be
   observed or measured about matter.

2. Matter can occur in three <u>mixtures</u>:
   solid, liquid, or gas.

3. The <u>boiling point</u> of a material is the
   temperature at which it changes from
   a solid to a liquid.

4. <u>Inertia</u> can cause objects to move,
   slow down, or stop.

5. Levers, inclined planes, and pulleys are
   examples of <u>closed circuits</u>.

6. A <u>series circuit</u> uses an energy source
   and a magnet to make electricity.

7. The magnetic field of a magnet is
   strongest at the <u>center</u> of the magnet.

8. A <u>transparent</u> object spreads light in
   different directions as the light passes
   through it.

9. When sound waves reach your ear,
   they make your <u>brain</u> vibrate.

10. A <u>bullhorn</u> is an instrument used to
    help people with a loss of hearing
    hear better.

Interpreting Data

The following graph shows the speed of sound through different materials. Use the graph to answer the questions below.

Speed of Sound

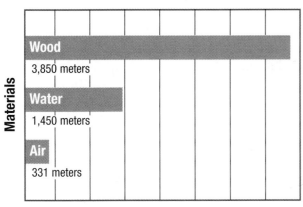

Materials

Wood
3,850 meters

Water
1,450 meters

Air
331 meters

0   500   1,000 1,500 2,000 2,500 3,000 3,500
Distance traveled in 1 second

1. Does sound travel faster through air or through wood?

2. How much faster does sound travel through water than through air?

3. If you wanted to soundproof a room, would you use wood, water, or air as insulation?

Communicating Science

1. Draw and label a diagram to show a chemical change.

2. Draw a picture of work being done and label it to explain the work. List five other examples of work being done.

3. Draw a series circuit and a parallel circuit. Describe how they are different from each other.

4. Draw and label a diagram that shows how sound travels through your ear. Explain what parts of the ear vibrate as the sound waves move through the ear.

Applying Science

1. Write a paragraph or draw a diagram to explain the physical changes and the chemical changes that happened to the food you ate for breakfast—before you ate it and afterward.

2. Write an advertisement from an electric company advising customers how to use electricity safely.

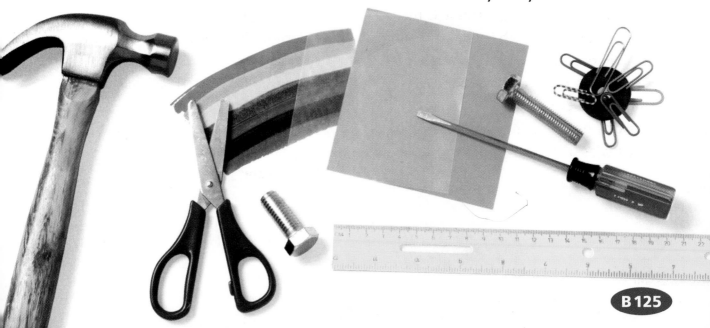

Unit B
Performance Review

Matter and Energy Museum

Using what you learned in this unit, complete one or more of the following activities to be included in a Matter and Energy Museum. These exhibits will help the visitors learn more about matter and energy. You may work by yourself or in a group.

New Invention

Think of a new way to combine two or more simple machines to do work. Draw a diagram and make a model of your machine. Then write an advertisement that tells what your machine can do to help make work easier. Display your machine in the museum.

Art

As part of a museum display, make a poster to show examples that explain the difference between physical changes and chemical changes. You may draw pictures or cut pictures from magazines.

Music and Dance

Plan a musical revue for the museum. Make up a song or a dance to show how sound travels through different kinds of materials. Plan to use instruments that you make—such as drums made from coffee cans—to accompany the song or dance.

Graphs

For the math room of the museum, make a graph to show some data you have collected about matter and energy. Display your graph and write a brief summary of what data the graph shows.

Electromagnets

Collect pictures or items that use electromagnets. Arrange them for display in your museum. Write tags to describe each item and tell how an electromagnet is used in the item.

Outlining and Writing a Report

An outline can help you organize your thoughts before you write. An outline lists the main ideas and the supporting details for the different sections or paragraphs of a report.

Each main idea on an outline is listed next to a Roman numeral, such as I, II, and III. All of the supporting details listed below a main idea are listed next to a letter, such as A, B, and C.

The sample outline below shows an outline for Chapter 3 of this unit.

Chapter 3: Electricity and Magnetism

I. **Electric Current**
   A. How objects get a charge
   B. How electric current flows

II. **Electric Circuits**
   A. How two types of circuits are different
   B. How electricity can be used safely

III. **Magnetism**
   A. How magnets act
   B. How the earth is like a magnet

IV. **How Electricity and Magnetism Work Together**
   A. How a magnet can make electricity
   B. How electricity can make a magnet
   C. How electromagnets are useful

Make an Outline

Use this model to write an outline for Chapter 4 of this unit. Use the lesson titles and the main ideas from each lesson to complete your outline.

Write a Report

Use the information from your Chapter 4 outline to write one sentence about what you learned for each of your main ideas. Then write one sentence about what you learned for each of your supporting details. Use transition words such as *first, next, then, because,* and *however* to shape groups of words into four paragraphs. Add a brief introduction and closing. Remember to give your report a title.

Remember to:

1. **Prewrite** Organize your thoughts before you write.

2. **Draft** Make an outline and write your report.

3. **Revise** Share your work and then make changes.

4. **Edit** Proofread for mistakes and fix them.

5. **Publish** Share your report with your class.

Your Science Handbook

Safety in Science

Scientists know they must work safely when doing experiments. You need to be careful when doing experiments too. The next page shows some safety tips to remember.

Safety Tips

- Read each experiment carefully.

- Wear safety goggles when needed.

- Clean up spills right away.

- Never taste or smell substances
  unless directed to do so by your teacher.

- Handle sharp items carefully.

- Tape sharp edges of materials.

- Handle thermometers carefully.

- Use chemicals carefully.

- Dispose of chemicals properly.

- Put materials away when you finish
  an experiment.

- Wash your hands after each experiment.

Using the Metric System

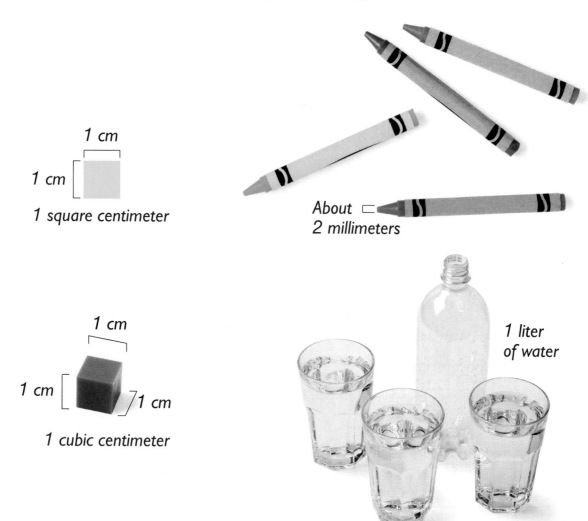

1 cm

1 cm

1 square centimeter

About 2 millimeters

1 cm

1 cm

1 cm

1 cubic centimeter

1 liter of water

11 football fields end to end is about 1 kilometer

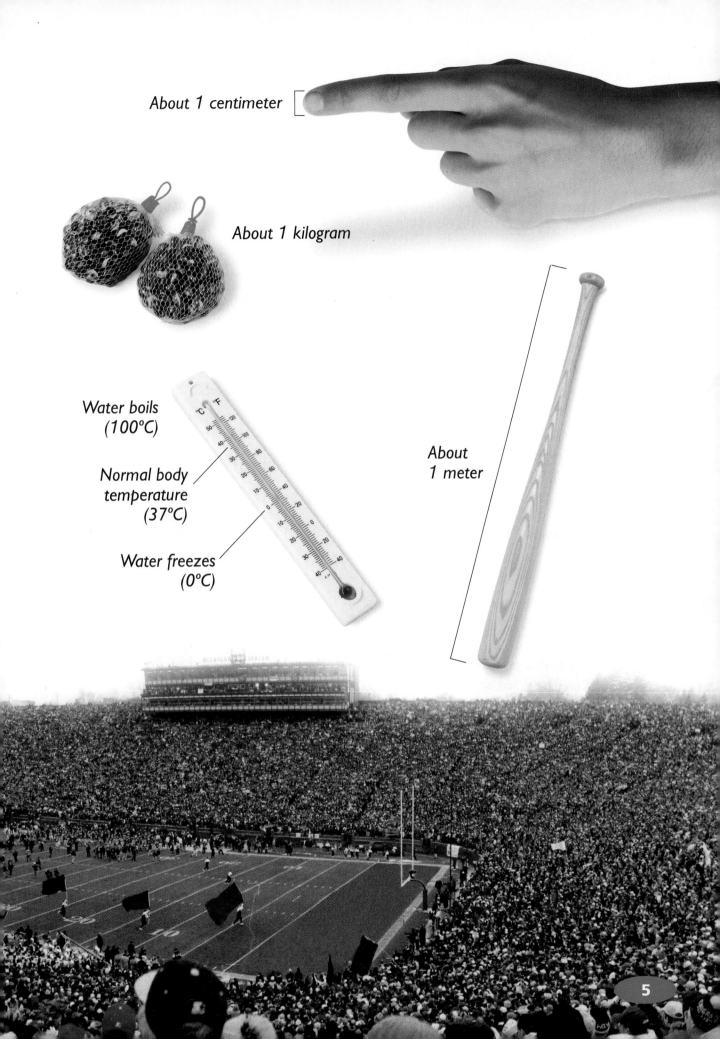

About 1 centimeter

About 1 kilogram

Water boils
(100°C)

Normal body
temperature
(37°C)

Water freezes
(0°C)

About
1 meter

Observing

How can you make accurate observations?

The process of observing is the most important of all the process skills. Every scientific investigation requires you to make accurate observations.

You must use all your senses—sight, touch, hearing, smelling, and taste—to find out about objects and events. You can pick up objects, feel them, shake them, press them, smell them, look at them, listen to them. Doing all these things will help you find out about objects.

Observing requires that you notice things or events that are changing. You must compare the properties of the objects or events before, during, and after the change.

You may use tools or measuring instruments to make better observations. Limit your observations to things that are directly related to your senses.

Practice Observing

Materials

- pencil
- paper
- tape measure
- hand lens

Follow This Procedure

1. Observe your pencil with as many senses as possible. Do not taste your pencil.

2. List each sense that you used and list your observations.

3. Notice things that are changing. Compare properties before, during, and after the change. For example, use your hand lens to look carefully at the "lead" in your pencil. It is graphite. Then scribble on a piece of paper. Describe how the graphite looked before, during, and after you scribbled on the paper.

4. Use tools to make better observations. Use a tape measure to make observations of your pencil. Make as many measurements as you can.

5. Describe only what you observe directly with your senses. Look over your list of observations and tell what sense you used to make each observation.

Thinking About Your Thinking

List the steps that you used to make accurate observations. What could you have done to make better observations?

Communicating

How can you communicate by using descriptions?

You communicate when you share information through words, pictures, charts, graphs, and diagrams. Each of these is a different way to communicate.

If you want to communicate about something that has many things to describe, you can use several different ways to express your observations. For example, you might make a map like the one shown. The map shows how to locate a treasure that is hidden on the island in the picture.

Practice Communicating

Materials

- ruler
- notebook
- pencil

Follow This Procedure

1. Begin a letter to a friend from another school, telling him or her that you will be describing your classroom.

2. Describe the light in the classroom. Is it mostly from the windows? What time of day is the window light brightest? Are there ceiling lights?

3. Describe the smell of the air. Does it smell like an old shoe? like flowers? like mouthwash?

4. Describe the color and texture of the walls. Does tape stick to it? Is the floor rough or smooth? Is it slippery?

5. Draw a map of the classroom. Include the doors, windows, blackboards, desks, and closets. Draw and label any special activity areas. Label your assigned seat if you have one.

6. Measure and describe the classroom by the "steps" method. First measure the length of your step in centimeters. Count how many steps it takes to cross the length of the classroom. Then count how many steps it takes to cross the width. Calculate the length of the classroom by multiplying the length of your steps by the number of steps necessary to cross its length. Use the same calculation to find the width. Record your results. In the letter you are writing, describe how your measurements were obtained.

7. Compare your letter with the letter of another student to discover what you may not have communicated.

Thinking About Your Thinking

How did creating a map improve the communication in your letter? Could you have described a complex environment like your classroom as well without it? Would it have taken a lot more words?

Think about how important it is for people to communicate the methods and units of measurement they are using. Is the "steps" method precise enough to communicate how to build parts for an airplane? What other ways to measure might you have used?

Classifying

How can you classify objects in nature?

You classify objects by arranging or grouping them according to their common properties. Practice classifying things in nature. It is important to use an organized way to classify.

Look at the leaves on this page. How are these leaves alike and different? How would you group these leaves according to their common properties?

Practice Classifying

Materials

- collection of six leaves
- small magnifying glass
- pencil

Follow This Procedure

1 Classify your collection of leaves by their different characteristics. Make a list of the characteristics you used.

2 How many different ways did you sort your collection? Why did you choose those characteristics?

3 Plant scientists, or botanists, classify leaves in many ways. Look at each of your leaves. Are they thin and needle-like? Are they broad, or wide?

4 Look at a broad leaf. Notice the little stem at the bottom. The rest of the leaf is called the *blade*. Veins run from the little stem into the blade. You can see them with or without your hand lens. Do the veins alternate off of one big vein in the middle? Do they all branch off from the stem? Do they run in straight lines without touching?

5 Classify your broad leaves as one of the following.

(1) having alternating veins
(2) having branching veins
(3) going in a straight line

Thinking About Your Thinking

Would you have thought about classifying leaves by their vein structure?

How else could you classify leaves? Could you have used color pattern? smell?

Estimating and Measuring

How can you estimate and measure a large number of objects?

An estimate is an intelligent, informed guess about an object's properties. Sometimes you may want to estimate how many objects are in a container without having to count or measure every object.

Suppose you were given the assignment to tell how many raisins were in a box of cereal. You surely wouldn't want to count every raisin. That would take too long. Instead you could decide on a plan to estimate and measure the cereal to come up with a reasonable answer.

Practice Estimating and Measuring

Materials

- 16 oz. box of raisin cereal
- measuring cup
- large bowl

Follow This Procedure

1 Work with a partner to estimate the number of raisins in the box of cereal.

2 Use the measuring cup to determine how many cups of cereal are in the box. Pour the cereal into the measuring cup and then put the cereal from the measuring cup into the bowl. Keep track of how many cups you poured into the bowl.

3 Divide the total number of cups in the box by 2. Round the answer up to the next whole number. Write down this number.

4 Use the measuring cup to take 2 cups of cereal back out of the bowl. Separate the raisins from the cereal. Count how many raisins were in the two cups of cereal.

5 Multiply the number of raisins in two cups of cereal by the number that you got in step 3. This will give you an estimate of the number of raisins in the whole box of cereal.

Thinking About Your Thinking

Can you think of another way to make a better estimate of the number of raisins in the box? Would taking a larger sample of cereal make any difference to the accuracy of your estimate? Try it to find out.

Inferring

How do you infer?

You infer when you make a reasonable guess, based on what you observe or on what you have experienced.

Observing with one or more of your senses—seeing, hearing, smelling, or touching—can be the reason for your inference. If you have done something in the past, what you learned can also help you make a good inference.

For example, when you watch TV or read a magazine, there are commercials or ads. You have seen these before and you know that someone is trying to sell you something. Watch a commercial. What do the advertisers want you to believe about their product?

Ad	Observation	Inference

Practice Inferring

Materials
- magazines or newspapers

Follow This Procedure

1. Make a chart like the one shown.

2. Look through a magazine or newspaper. Cut out several ads.

3. Read these ads carefully. List an observation and an inference that could be made about the ad.

4. Draw a conclusion about these ads. Is the message that the advertiser was trying to send accurate? Why or why not?

Thinking About Your Thinking

Watch several commercials on television. How do the commercials compare to the ads in the magazine or newspaper? Which type of advertising is more likely to make you want to buy a product—ads or TV commercials? Why do you think this is so?

Predicting

How can you make accurate predictions?

Predicting is an important process skill. There are five steps to making accurate predictions.

1. Make observations and measurements. Remember what you learned from doing something in the past.

2. Search for patterns in the data. Make inferences.

3. Make predictions about what may happen in the future. Use your inferences.

4. Test your predictions.

5. After testing, revise your predictions if necessary.

Practice Predicting

Materials

- meter stick
- small rubber ball

Follow This Procedure

1 Make a chart like the one below.

Drop	Predictions	Bounces
25 cm	X	
30 cm	X	
50 cm		
75 cm		
100 cm		

2 Work with a partner. Have your partner hold the meter stick with the 100 cm at the top.

3 Drop the ball from the 25 centimeter line on the meter stick. Have your partner count how many times the ball bounces.

4 Repeat this activity from the 30 centimeter line. Record the number of bounces.

5 Predict how many times the ball will bounce from the 50, 75, and 100 centimeter lines.

6 Do the activity and record the number of times the ball bounces from the 50, 75, and 100 centimeter lines.

Thinking About Your Thinking

How accurate were your predictions? What information did you use to make your predictions? If you dropped the ball from 200 centimeters, what would your prediction for the number of bounces be? Why?

Making Operational Definitions

How do you write an operational definition?

An operational definition is a definition or description of an object or an event based on your experience with it. As you gain experience with an object or event, your operational definition of it may become more effective. Keep your operational definition as simple as possible. Can you write an operational definition for the word "electricity"? Remember, use what you know already to write the definition. Do not look it up in a dictionary.

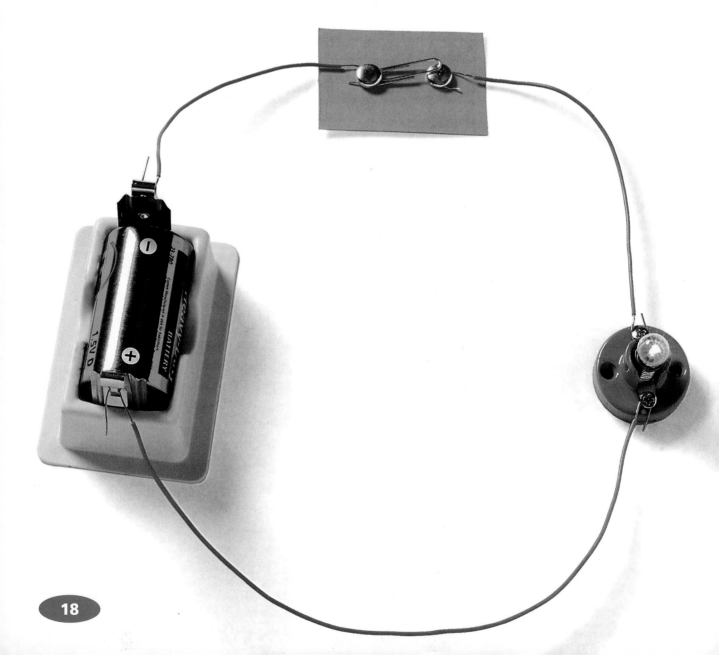

Practice Making Operational Definitions

Materials

- 1 D-cell battery
- 1 flashlight bulb
- insulated wire—both ends stripped

Follow This Procedure

1. Look at the diagram of the closed circuit. Set up the bulb, battery, and wire to make a closed circuit so the bulb lights.

2. Write your definition of a closed circuit based on what you did.

3. Look up *circuit* in your science book or the dictionary and write the definition given in the book.

4. How is your definition of a circuit different from the definition given in the book?

Thinking About Your Thinking

How did making a closed circuit help you define it? How did your definition communicate what the closed circuit did?

Making and Using Models

How can making a model help you understand a difficult concept?

There are many things to learn in your science book. Some of those things are easier to understand if you can see the object or event. You can make a model or copy of many of the objects or events in science.

For example, you can't go to a desert, forest, or prairie to see how animals live in these environments. However, you can build dioramas in shoeboxes or make posters of animals in their habitats. These models help you learn about animals and their habitats.

Practice Making and Using Models

Materials

- clear tape
- pictures of animals from magazines, web sites, or student drawings
- 4 different pieces of construction paper
- large poster board

Follow This Procedure

1. Cut out or draw pictures of 4 animals that go together in a food chain.

2. Tape these animals on the 4 different pieces of construction paper.

3. Put the pictures in order on the poster board.

4. Label the food chain, showing the direction that it goes.

5. Write a description of the food chain that you created for your class.

6. Create a series of questions that go with your food chain. Have your classmates answer these questions. Examples might be:

   What is the source of energy for the ____?

   What does the ____ eat?

   Which animal or organism starts the food chain?

   What do you think would happen to the ____ if it couldn't eat the ____?

Thinking About Your Thinking

Why do you think that the model that you made is called a "chain"? What other models could you make that might help explain what a food chain is?

Formulating Questions and Hypotheses

How do you formulate relevant questions and hypotheses?

The scientific process often begins when you ask yourself a question to solve a problem. You then formulate statements, or hypotheses, so you can test them. From the results of the test, you may be able to answer the question or to solve the problem.

When scientists form a possible answer to a question, they also form a hypothesis. For example, "If I do this ... then this will happen."

Practice Formulating Questions and Hypotheses

Materials

- 6 straws
- scissors
- tape
- piece of construction paper

Follow This Procedure

1 Question: How does the length of the straw affect the pitch of the sound produced?

2 Cut one end of a straw to form a point and blow into this end of the straw to produce a sound. Observe the pitch of the sound produced (high or low).

3 Write a hypothesis about the length of the straw and its pitch.

4 Trim the 5 remaining straws to different lengths. Then cut one end of each straw to form a point. Blow into this end and observe the pitch of the sound produced.

5 Arrange your 6 straws in order from the highest to the lowest pitch and tape the straws on a piece of construction paper.

Thinking About Your Thinking

Did your investigation prove that your hypothesis is correct?

As you observe at school and home, think about questions you would like to find out about. Practice forming hypotheses to answer your questions. How would you test each hypothesis?

Collecting and Interpreting Data

How do you collect and interpret data accurately?

You collect and interpret data when you gather measurements and organize them into graphs, tables, charts, or diagrams. You can then use the information to solve problems or to answer questions.

When people take surveys, they ask many questions and collect a lot of useful data. This information is then put into charts and graphs so it's easier to understand. Have you ever taken a survey?

1. What color eyes do you have? _____

2. What color hair do you have? _____

3. How many brothers and sisters do you have? _____

Practice Collecting and Interpreting Data

Materials

- pencil
- paper

Follow This Procedure

1 Make a chart like the one below to record how many of your classmates have blue eyes, brown eyes, or green eyes.

Eye Color	Tally of Students	Totals
Blue		
Brown		
Green		

2 Make a chart like the one below to record how many of your classmates have blonde hair, red hair, brown hair, or black hair.

Hair Color	Tally of Students	Totals
Blonde		
Red		
Brown		
Black		

3 Take a survey to collect data on hair color and eye color from each of your classmates. Make a tally mark for each student's answer in the correct place on the charts. Then calculate the total number of students that chose each answer.

4 Which hair color do most students have? Which eye color do most students have?

Thinking About Your Thinking

What other questions might you have included on your survey? Is a chart the best way to show this data? Why or why not?

Identifying and Controlling Variables

How do you identify and control variables?

You identify and control variables when you change one factor that may affect the outcome of an event while keeping all other factors the same.

The first step is to determine which variable you want to change. You must also identify the variables you want to keep the same.

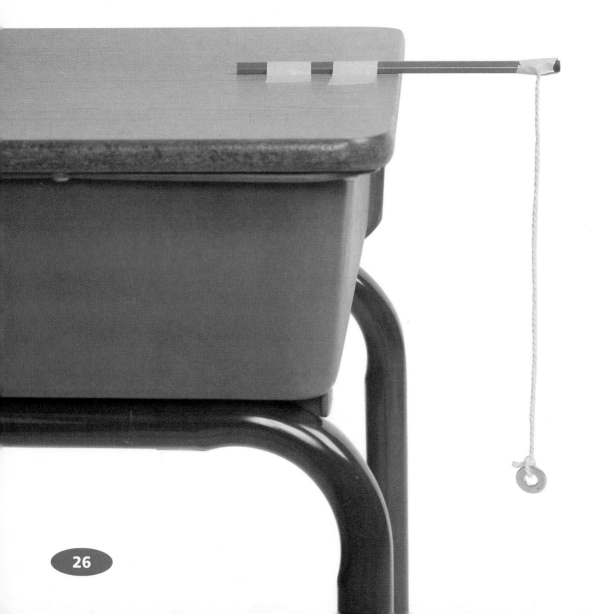

Practice Identifying and Controlling Variables

Materials

- string
- scissors
- metric ruler
- 6 washers
- pencil
- tape
- timer or watch with second hand

Follow This Procedure

1 Make a chart like the one below.

Length of Pendulum	Number of Swings
60 cm	
50 cm	
40 cm	
30 cm	
20 cm	
10 cm	

2 Cut the string into 6 pieces of the following lengths: 60 cm, 50 cm, 40 cm, 30 cm, 20 cm, 10 cm. Tie a washer to the end of each piece of string.

3 Tape the pencil to the table so that about 3 cm hangs over the edge. Tape the 60 cm pendulum onto the pencil. Hold the washer even with the top of the table and release it.

4 Count how many times the pendulum swings back and forth in 15 seconds, and record the number of swings in the chart.

5 Repeat this procedure with the other five pendulums.

Thinking About Your Thinking

Which variable did you change? Which variable responded to the change (what did you count)? Which variables were kept constant? How does the length of the pendulum affect the number of times it swings in 15 seconds?

27

Experimenting

What does scientific experimenting involve?

Scientific experimenting involves making a plan to test a hypothesis and then forming a conclusion based on the results.

The first step is to write the problem you are investigating and come up with a hypothesis.

Next, think how you should organize, or design, the investigation. Which variables will you keep constant? What one variable will you decide to change?

Next, perform the experiment to test your hypothesis. Accurate record keeping is another important part of experimenting. You should record your procedure and data accurately so that you and others can repeat the experiment.

Practice Experimenting

Materials

- masking tape
- magnets of different strengths
- paper clips

Follow This Procedure

1 Use the masking tape to label the magnets 1 and 2. Look at the two magnets. Can you tell which magnet will pick up the most paper clips?

2 State the problem. Which magnet is stronger?

3 Write a hypothesis about which magnet you think will pick up more paper clips.

4 Design your experiment. The variable that changes is the magnet. Are the paper clips a variable that changes?

5 Construct a chart like the one below to show your results.

Number of Paper Clips Picked Up	
Magnet 1	
Magnet 2	

6 Perform the experiment.

7 Make a grid for a bar graph like the one below. Graph your results.

8 Compare your hypothesis with the results. State your conclusion.

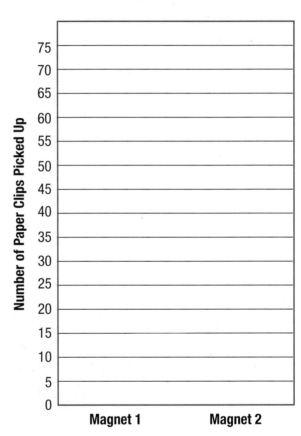

Thinking About Your Thinking

What did you learn from this experiment?

Systems

A system is a set of things that form a whole. Systems can be made of many different parts. All the parts depend on each other and work together. Systems can have living things and nonliving things.

The schoolyard on the next page is an example of a system that contains living things. Parts of the system that interact and depend on each other are the students, the grass, the bee, the clover plant, and the dandelion plant.

The circuit below is a nonliving system. The light bulb, the wires, the switch, and the energy source all make up the system.

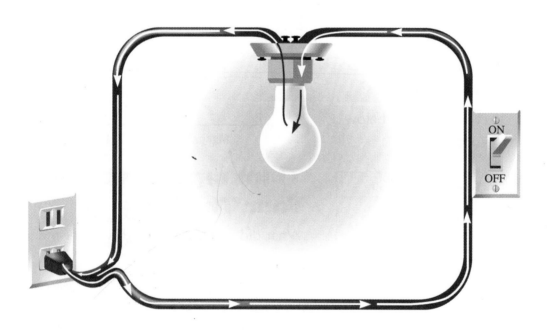

Layers of the Earth

Atmosphere

A blanket of air, called the atmosphere, surrounds the earth. The earth's atmosphere protects it from harmful sunlight and helps organisms on the earth survive.

Crust

The earth itself is made of layers. The outer layer, or crust, of the earth is made up of rocks and soil. The land you walk on and the land under the oceans are part of the crust.

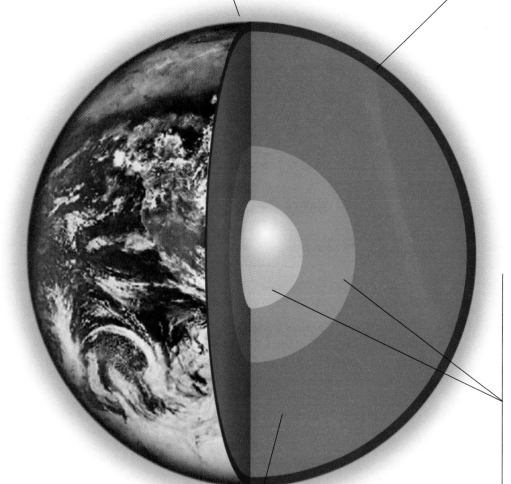

Core

The center of the earth—the core—is made mostly of iron. The outside part of the core has liquid iron. The inside part has solid iron. The core is the hottest part of the earth. The temperature of the core is almost as hot as the surface of the sun!

Mantle

The middle layer of the earth is called the mantle. The mantle is mostly made of rock. Some of the rock in the mantle is partly melted.

Climate Zones

A climate is the weather conditions which describe an area over many years. The earth has three basic climate zones—tropical, temperate, and polar. Areas within these zones can have different climates. Across the United States, climates vary because of differences in the amount of rainfall and temperature. There are no clear boundary lines between climate areas in the United States.

Highland climate
The highland climate mountain zones have very cold winters and cool summers.

Grassland climate
A grassland climate gets little rainfall during the year. This zone has very cold temperatures and snow in winter and hot temperatures in the summer.

Humid continental climate
A humid continental climate has warm summers with a lot of rain. Winters are very cold with a lot of snow.

Humid subtropical climate
The humid subtropical climate has long, warm, moist summers, followed by mild winters.

Mediterranean climate
Summers in a Mediterranean climate are very dry with mild temperatures. Winters are wet with mild temperatures.

Desert climate
A desert climate receives very little rain during the year. It is usually much hotter during the day than at night.

Tundra

Subarctic

Tropical

The Rock Cycle

In the rock cycle, rocks form and change into other types of rock. Rocks form in three main ways. Over millions of years, each type of rock can change into another type of rock.

Rocks that form from melted material deep inside the earth are igneous rocks. Granite is an igneous rock.

As a result of weathering, rocks break down. Sand and small bits of rock sink beneath the water. Layers of material press together underwater and form sedimentary rocks. Sandstone is a sedimentary rock.

Metamorphic rock forms as very high heat and great pressure within the earth change igneous and sedimentary rocks. Gneiss is a metamorphic rock.

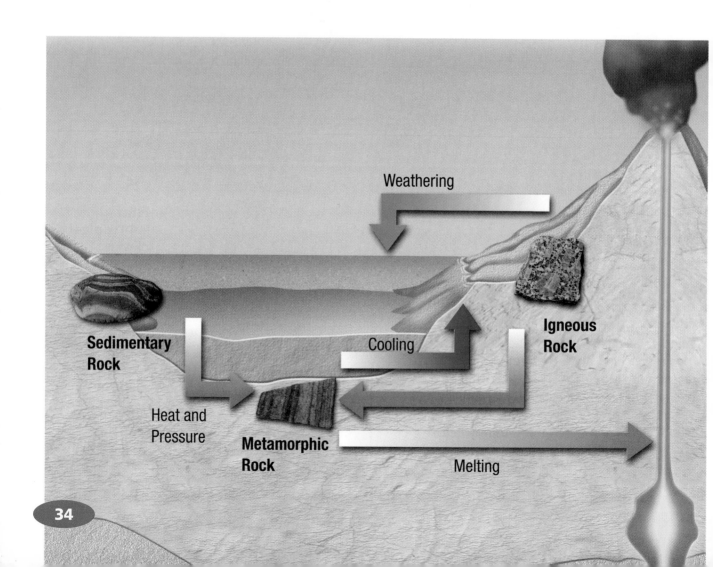

Weathering

Sedimentary
Rock

Cooling

Igneous
Rock

Heat and
Pressure

Metamorphic
Rock

Melting

Minerals

In 1822, Frederich Mohs created a scale that showed the hardness of certain minerals. On his scale, minerals with higher numbers are harder than minerals with lower numbers. You can tell how hard a mineral is by rubbing it against another mineral. The harder mineral will scratch the softer mineral. A diamond is the hardest mineral known. It will scratch any other mineral.

Mohs' Scale of Hardness

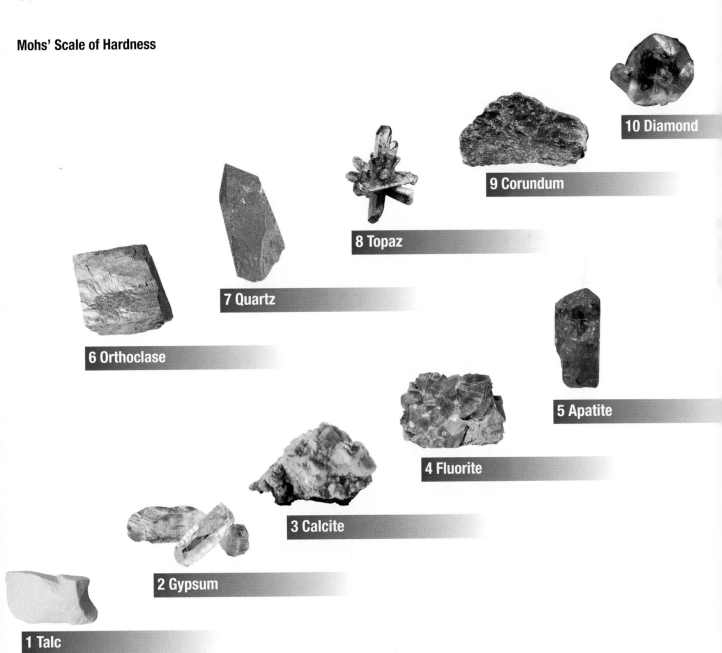

10 Diamond

9 Corundum

8 Topaz

7 Quartz

6 Orthoclase

5 Apatite

4 Fluorite

3 Calcite

2 Gypsum

1 Talc

Evidence of the Past

Many different types of organisms have existed on the earth throughout millions of years. Many types of organisms that lived millions of years ago are now extinct. Fossils of extinct organisms show that some plants and animals that lived long ago look very much like plants and animals that live today.

▲ *The woolly mammoth from thousands of years ago is similar to the elephant of today. The mammoth is now extinct.*

◀ *Scientists think that ferns date back hundreds of millions of years, making them some of the oldest types of plants on the earth.*

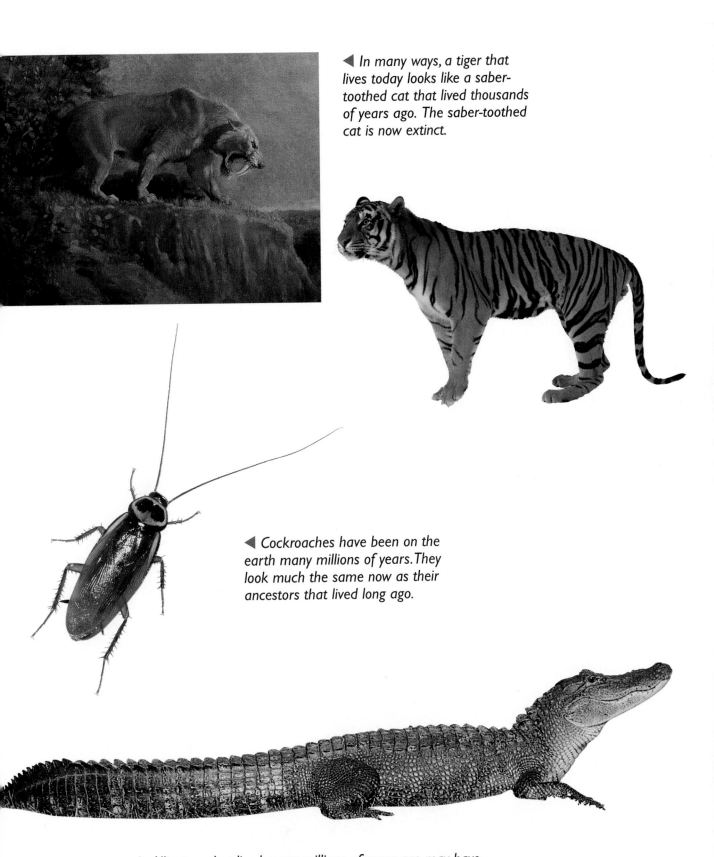

◀ In many ways, a tiger that lives today looks like a saber-toothed cat that lived thousands of years ago. The saber-toothed cat is now extinct.

◀ Cockroaches have been on the earth many millions of years. They look much the same now as their ancestors that lived long ago.

▲ Alligators that lived many millions of years ago may have been longer than alligators that live today. However, ancient alligators looked very much like alligators that live today.

Vertebrates and Invertebrates

The animal kingdom can be divided into two main groups. One group contains animals that have a backbone. Animals that have backbones are called vertebrates. The other group contains animals that do not have a backbone. These animals are called invertebrates.

▲ Crabs belong to a group called crustaceans.

Invertebrates

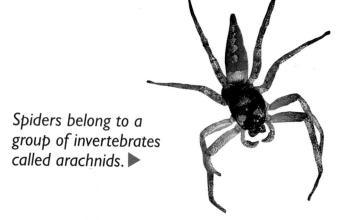

Spiders belong to a group of invertebrates called arachnids.▶

Earthworms are annelids. ▼

▲ Insects are the largest group of animals.

The group to which sponges belong is known as porifera. ▼

◀ Jellyfish are coelenterates.

Vertebrates

◀ Snakes, turtles, and lizards belong to a group called reptiles.

▲ A hummingbird is one of many different birds.

Koalas are mammals. ▶

Frogs are amphibians. ▶

Sharks are fishes. ▶

Life Cycles

Every living thing has a life cycle. In its life cycle, an organism goes through stages in which it grows, changes, and reproduces. Some young animals have the same body form as their parents. Others, such as frogs and butterflies, go through a metamorphosis, meaning they change form as they grow.

Life Cycle of a Frog

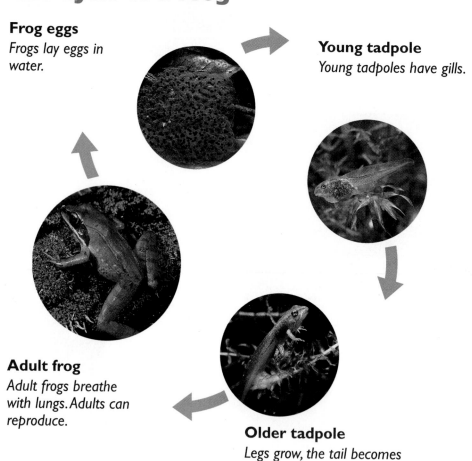

Frog eggs
Frogs lay eggs in water.

Young tadpole
Young tadpoles have gills.

Adult frog
Adult frogs breathe with lungs. Adults can reproduce.

Older tadpole
Legs grow, the tail becomes smaller, and lungs develop.

Life Cycle of a Butterfly

Egg
Butterflies lay their eggs on leaves.

Larva
The butterfly larva is also called a caterpillar.

Pupa
The larva wraps itself in a covering. The larva becomes a pupa. Its body changes form.

Butterfly
The covering opens and the butterfly comes out. After a time, the butterfly lays eggs. The cycle starts again.

Life Cycle of a Tree

Seeds
A seed falls to the ground.

Germination
A seed germinates when the tiny plant inside it begins to grow.

Fully grown tree
A fully grown plant makes flowers and seeds.

Seedling
A seedling is a young plant.

Cells, Tissues, Organs, and Body Systems

The human body is made of small units that join together to form larger and more complicated units.

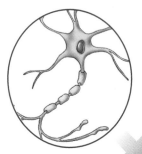

◀ *A cell is the basic unit of an organism. The body has many different kinds of cells. Each kind of cell does a different job. This cell is a nerve cell.*

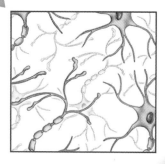

◀ *A group of the same kind of cells forms a tissue. A group of bone cells forms bone tissue, and a group of muscle cells forms muscle tissue. This diagram shows how nerve cells form nervous tissue.*

▶ *A group of many kinds of tissues forms an organ. The tissues in an organ work together to keep an organism alive. The brain is an organ that is made mainly of nervous tissue, but also has blood and other tissues.*

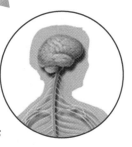

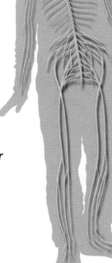

▶ *Different organs work together to do a job in the body. The organs that work together to do a special job make up a system. The brain, spinal cord, and nerves make up the nervous system.*

Body Systems

Each system in the human body has a special job to do.

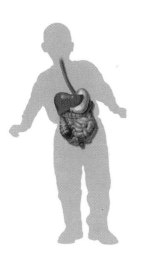

▲ Digestive System
This system changes food into a form that body cells can use.

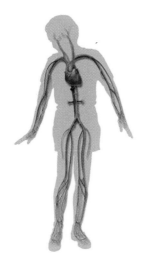

▲ Circulatory System
This system brings oxygen and nutrients to cells and takes away wastes.

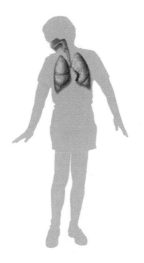

▲ Respiratory System
This system brings oxygen into the body and gives off waste gases.

▲ Nervous System
The brain and nerves control everything the body does.

▲ Excretory System
This system carries waste products out of the body.

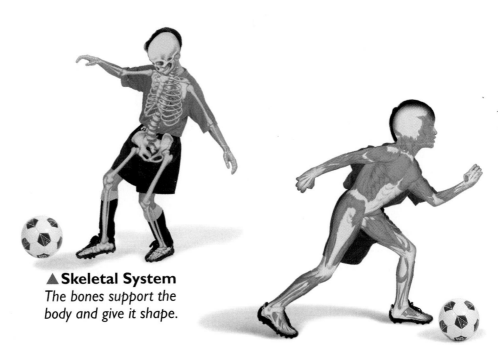

▲ Skeletal System
The bones support the body and give it shape.

▲ Muscular System
Muscles make body parts move and give the body shape.

Plant and Animal Cells

A cell is the smallest part that makes up a living thing. Plant and animal cells are different in some ways and alike in others. An animal cell contains a cell membrane, a nucleus, and cytoplasm. A plant cell contains a cell membrane, a nucleus, cytoplasm, a cell wall, and chloroplasts.

Animal Cell

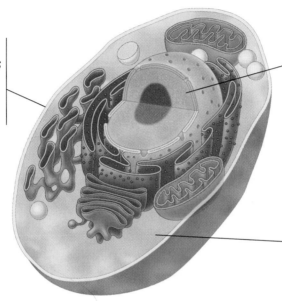

Cell Membrane
The cell membrane controls what goes in and out of the cell.

Nucleus
The nucleus directs the way the cell grows, develops, and divides.

Cytoplasm
Jellylike cytoplasm fills the cell and surrounds the nucleus.

Plant Cell

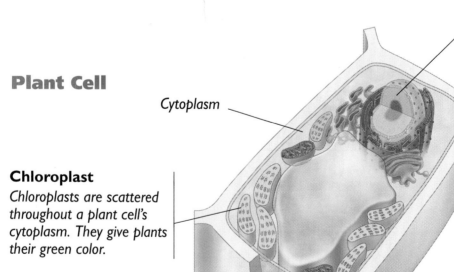

Nucleus

Cytoplasm

Chloroplast
Chloroplasts are scattered throughout a plant cell's cytoplasm. They give plants their green color.

Cell membrane

Cell Wall
A stiff wall surrounds a plant cell just outside its cell membrane. It keeps the cell rigid and helps the whole plant keep its shape.

Tools

Tools can make objects appear larger. They can help you measure volume, temperature, length, distance, and mass. Tools can help you figure out amounts and analyze your data. Tools can also provide you with the latest scientific information.

You can figure amounts using a calculator. ▶

▲ *Safety goggles protect your eyes.*

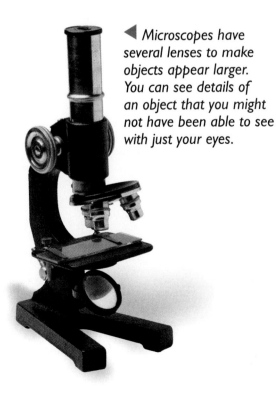

◀ *Microscopes have several lenses to make objects appear larger. You can see details of an object that you might not have been able to see with just your eyes.*

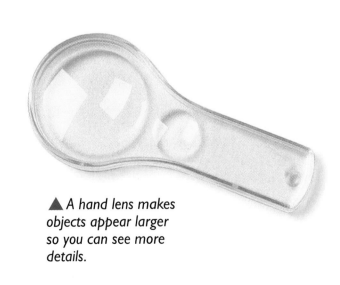

▲ *A hand lens makes objects appear larger so you can see more details.*

▲ Computers can quickly provide the latest scientific information.

▶ You use a thermometer to measure temperature. Many thermometers have both Farenheit and Celsius scales. Usually scientists only use the Celsius scale when measuring temperature.

Scientists use metric rulers and meter sticks to measure length and distance. Scientists use the metric units of meters, centimeters, and millimeters to measure length and distance. ▼

Pictures taken with a camera record what something looks like. You can compare pictures of the same object to show how the object might have changed. ▼

Clocks and stopwatches are used for measuring time. ▶

You can talk into a tape recorder to record information you want to remember. You can also use a tape recorder to record different sounds. ▲

▲ *You use a balance to measure mass.*

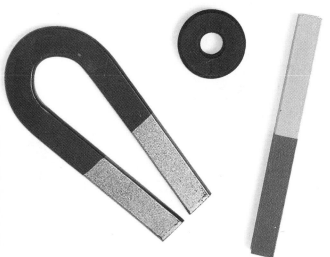

▲ *You can use a magnet to test whether an object is made of certain metals such as iron.*

▲*A compass is used to indicate direction. The directions on a compass include north, south, east, and west.*

History of Science

8000 B.C.	6000 B.C.	4000 B.C	2000 B.C.

Life Science

Physical Science

● **3000 B.C.**
The Egyptians develop geometry. They use it to re-measure their farmlands after floods of the Nile River.

Earth Science

● **8000 B.C.** Farming communities start as people use the plow for farming.

Human Body

4th century B.C.
Aristotle classifies
plants and animals.

3rd century B.C.
Aristarchus proposes that the
earth revolves around the sun.

4th century B.C.
Aristotle describes the
motions of falling
bodies. He believes that
heavier things fall faster
than lighter things.

260 B.C. Archimedes
discovers the principles of
buoyancy and the lever.

4th century B.C. Aristotle
describes the motions
of the planets.

200 B.C. Eratosthenes calculates
the size of the earth. His result is
very close to the earth's actual
size.

87 B.C.
Chinese report observing
an object in the sky that
later became known as
Halley's comet.

5th and 4th centuries B.C.
Hippocrates and other Greek
doctors record the symptoms of
many diseases. They also urge
people to eat a well-balanced diet.

**Life
Science**

**Physical
Science**

83 A.D.
Chinese travelers
use the compass
for navigation.

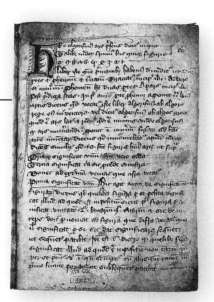

About
750–1250
Islamic scholars get
scientific books
from Europe. They
translate them into
Arabic and add
more information.

**Earth
Science**

140 Claudius Ptolemy
draws a complete picture of
an earth-centered universe.

132 The Chinese make the
first seismograph, a device
that measures the strength
of earthquakes.

**Human
Body**

2nd century Galen
writes about anatomy
and the causes of
diseases.

1100s
Animal guide books begin to appear. They describe what animals look like and give facts about them.

1250
Albert the Great describes plants and animals in his book *On Vegetables and On Animals*.

1555
Pierre Belon finds similarities between the skeletons of humans and birds.

9th century
The Chinese invent block printing. By the 11th century, they had movable type.

1019
Abu Arrayhan Muhammad ibn Ahmad al'Biruni observed both a solar and lunar eclipse within a few months of each other.

1543
Nikolaus Copernicus publishes his book *On The Revolutions of the Celestial Orbs*. It says that the sun remains still and the earth moves in a circle around it.

1265
Nasir al-Din al-Tusi gets his own observatory. His ideas about how the planets move will influence Nikolaus Copernicus.

About 1000
Ibn Sina writes an encyclopedia of medical knowledge. For many years, doctors will use this as their main source of medical knowledge. Arab scientist Ibn Al-Haytham gives the first detailed explanation of how we see and how light forms images in our eyes.

1543
Andreas Vesalius publishes *On the Makeup of the Human Body*. In this book he gives very detailed pictures of human anatomy.

51

Life Science

1663 Robert Hooke first sees the cells of living organisms through a microscope. Antoni van Leeuwenhoek discovers bacteria with the microscope in 1674.

1679 Maria Sibylla Merian paints the first detailed pictures of a caterpillar turning into a butterfly. She also develops new techniques for printing pictures.

Physical Science

1600 William Gilbert describes the behavior of magnets. He also shows that the attraction of a compass needle toward North is due to the earth's magnetic pole.

1632 Galileo Galilei shows that all objects fall at the same speed. Galileo also shows that all matter has inertia.

1687 Isaac Newton introduces his three laws of motion.

Earth Science

1609–1619 Johannes Kepler introduces the three laws of planetary motion.

1610 Galileo uses a telescope to see the rings around the planet Saturn and the moons of Jupiter.

1669 Nicolaus Steno sets forth the basic principles of how to date rock layers.

1650 Maria Cunitz publishes a new set of tables to help astronomers find the positions of the planets and stars.

1693–1698 Maria Eimmart draws 250 pictures depicting the phases of the moon. She also paints flowers and insects.

1687 Isaac Newton introduces the concept of gravity.

Human Body

1628 William Harvey shows how the heart circulates blood through the blood vessels.

1735 Carolus Linnaeus devises the modern system of naming living things.

1704 Isaac Newton publishes his views on optics. He shows that white light contains many colors.

1759 Emile du Châtelet translates Isaac Newton's work into French. Her work still remains the only French translation.

1789 Antoine-Laurent Lavoisier claims that certain substances, such as oxygen, hydrogen, and nitrogen, cannot be broken down into anything simpler. He calls these substances "elements."

1729 Stephen Gray shows that electricity flows in a straight path from one place to another.

1781 Caroline and William Herschel (sister and brother) discover the planet Uranus.

1784 French chemist Antoine-Laurent Lavoisier does the first extensive study of respiration.

1798 Edward Jenner reports the first successful vaccination for smallpox.

1721 Onesimus introduces to America the African method for inoculation against smallpox.

1805	1810	1815	1820	1825	1830	1835

Life Science

1808 French naturalist Georges Cuvier describes some fossilized bones as belonging to a giant, extinct marine lizard.

1838–1839 Matthias Schleiden and Theodor Schwann describe the cell as the basic unit of a living organism.

Physical Science

1800 Alessandro Volta makes the first dry cell (battery).

1820 H.C. Oersted discovers that a wire with electric current running through it will deflect a compass needle. This showed that electricity and magnetism were related.

1808 John Dalton proposes that all matter is made of atoms.

Earth Science

1830 Charles Lyell writes *Principles of Geology*. This is the first modern geology textbook.

1803 Luke Howard assigns to clouds the basic names that we still use today— cumulus, stratus, and cirrus.

Human Body

1842 Richard Owen gives the name "dinosaurs" to the extinct giant lizards.

1859 Charles Darwin proposes the theory of evolution by natural selection.

1863 Gregor Mendel shows that certain traits in peas are passed to succeeding generations in a regular fashion. He outlines the methods of heredity.

1847 Hermann Helmholtz states the law of conservation of energy. This law holds that energy cannot be created or destroyed. Energy only can be changed from one form to another.

1842 Christian Doppler explains why a car, train, plane, or any quickly moving object sounds higher pitched as it approaches and lower pitched as it moves away.

1866 Ernst Haeckel proposes the term "ecology" for the study of the environment.

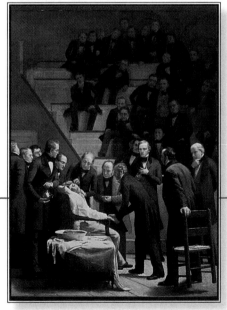

Early 1860s Louis Pasteur realizes that tiny organisms cause wine and milk to turn sour. He shows that heating the liquids kills these germs. This process is called pasteurization.

1840s Doctors use anesthetic drugs to put their patients to sleep.

1850s and 1860s Ignaz P. Semmelweis and Sir Joseph Lister pioneer the use of antiseptics in medicine.

Life Science

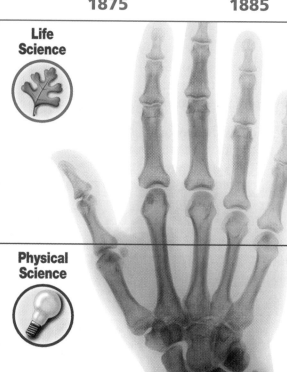

● **1900–1910** George Washington Carver, the son of slave parents, develops many new uses for old crops. He finds a way to make soybeans into rubber, cotton into road-paving material, and peanuts into paper.

Physical Science

● **1897**
J. J. Thomson discovers the electron.

1895 ●
Wilhelm Roentgen discovers X rays.

1896 Henri ●
Becquerel discovers radioactivity.

● **1905**
Albert Einstein introduces the theory of relativity.

Earth Science

1907 ●
Bertram Boltwood introduces the idea of "radioactive" dating. This allows geologists to accurately measure the age of a fossil.

1912 ●
Alfred Wegener proposes the theory of continental drift. This theory says that all land on the earth was once a single mass. It eventually broke apart and the continents slowly drifted away from each other.

Human Body

● **1885** Louis Pasteur gives the first vaccination for rabies. Pasteur thought that tiny organisms caused most diseases.

1920s Ernest Everett Just performs important research into how cells metabolize food.

1947 Archaeologist Mary Leakey unearths the skull of a *Proconsul africanus,* an example of a fossilized ape.

1913 Danish physicist Niels Bohr presents the modern theory of the atom.

1911 Ernst Rutherford discovers that atoms have a nucleus, or center.

1911 Marie Curie wins the Nobel Prize for chemistry. This makes her the first person ever to win two Nobel Prizes, the highest award a scientist can receive.

1938 Otto Hahn and Fritz Straussman split the uranium atom. This marks the beginning of the nuclear age.

1942 Enrico Fermi and Leo Szilard produce the first nuclear chain reaction.

1945 The first atomic bomb is exploded in the desert at Alamogordo, New Mexico.

1938 Lise Meitner and Otto Frisch explain how an atom can split in two.

1946 Vincent Schaefer and Irving Langmuir use dry ice to produce the first artificial rain.

1933 Meteorologist Tor Bergeron explains how raindrops form in clouds.

1917 Florence Sabin becomes the first woman professor at an American medical college.

1928 Alexander Fleming notices that the molds in his petri dish produced a substance, later called an antibiotic, that killed bacteria. He calls this substance penicillin.

1935 Chemist Percy Julian develops physostigmine, a drug used to fight the eye disease glaucoma.

1922 Doctors inject the first diabetes patient with insulin.

1950	1955	1960	1965	1970

Life Science

1951 Barbara McClintock discovers that genes can move to different places on a chromosome.

1953 The collective work of James D. Watson, Francis Crick, Maurice Wilkins, and Rosalind Franklin leads to the discovery of the structure of the DNA molecule.

1972 Researchers find human DNA to be 99% similar to that of chimpanzees.

Physical Science

1969 UCLA is host to the first computer node of ARPANET, the forerunner of the internet.

1974 Opening of TRIUMF, the world's largest particle accelerator, at the University of British Columbia.

Earth Science

1957 The first human-made object goes into orbit when the Soviet Union launches *Sputnik I.*

1969 Neil Armstrong is the first person to walk on the moon.

1972 Cygnus X-1 is first identified as a blackhole.

1967 Geophysicists introduce the theory of plate tectonics.

1962 John Glenn is the first American to orbit the earth.

Human Body

1954–1962 In 1954, Jonas Salk introduced the first vaccine for polio. In 1962, most doctors and hospitals substituted Albert Sabin's orally administered vaccine.

1967 Dr. Christiaan Barnard performs the first successful human heart transplant operation.

1964 The surgeon general's report on the hazards of smoking is released.

NO SMOKING
American Cancer Society

1988 Congress approves funding for the Human Genome Project. This project will map and sequence the human genetic code.

1997 Scientists in Edinburgh, Scotland, successfully clone a sheep, Dolly.

1975 People are able to buy the first personal computer, called the Altair.

1996 Scientists make "element 112" in the laboratory. This is the heaviest element yet created.

1979 A near meltdown occurs at the Three Mile Island nuclear power plant in Pennsylvania. This alerts the nation to the dangers of nuclear power.

1976 National Academy of Sciences reports on the dangers of chlorofluorocarbons (CFCs) for the earth's ozone layer.

1995 The first "extra-solar" planet is discovered.

Early 1990s The National Severe Storms Laboratory develops NEXRAD, the national network of Doppler weather radar stations for early severe storm warnings.

1981 The first commercial Magnetic Resonance Imaging scanners are available. Doctors use MRI scanners to look at the non-bony parts of the body.

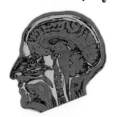

1982 Dr. Stanley Prusiner identifies a new kind of disease-causing agent—prions. Prions are responsible for many brain disorders.

1998 John Glenn, age 77, orbits the earth aboard the space shuttle *Discovery*. Glenn is the oldest person to fly in space.

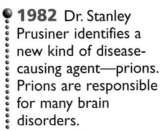

Glossary

Full Pronunciation Key

The pronunciation of each word is shown just after the word, in this way: **ab•bre•vi•ate** (ə brē′vē āt).

The letters and signs used are pronounced as in the words below.

The mark ′ is placed after a syllable with primary or heavy accent, as in the example above.

The mark ′ after a syllable shows a secondary or lighter accent, as in **ab•bre•vi•a•tion** (ə brē′vē ā′shən).

a	hat, cap	g	go, bag	ō	open, go	ᴛʜ	then,	zh	measure,
ā	age, face	h	he, how	ȯ	all, caught		smooth		seizure
â	care, fair	i	it, pin	ô	order	u	cup, butter		
ä	father, far	ī	ice, five	oi	oil, voice	u̇	full, put	ə	represents:
b	bad, rob	j	jam, enjoy	ou	house, out	ü	rule, move		a in about
ch	child, much	k	kind, seek	p	paper, cup	v	very, save		e in taken
d	did, red	l	land, coal	r	run, try	w	will,		i in pencil
e	let, best	m	me, am	s	say, yes		woman		o in lemon
ē	equal, be	n	no, in	sh	she, rush	y	young, yet		u in circus
ėr	term, learn	ng	long, bring	t	tell, it	z	zero,		
f	fat, if	o	hot, rock	th	thin, both		breeze		

A

absorb (ab sôrb′), to take in.

adaptation (ad′ap tā′shən), any structure or behavior that helps a living thing meet its need for survival.

air mass (âr mas), a large body of air that has about the same temperature and humidity throughout.

air pressure (âr presh′ər), the amount that air presses or pushes on anything.

amphibian (am fib′ē ən), one of a large group of animals with backbones that live part of their lives in water and part on land.

amplify (am′plə fī), to make stronger.

anemia (ə nē′mē ə), a condition in which the number of healthy red blood cells or the amount of hemoglobin is low.

anemometer (an′ə mom′ə tər), a tool that measures wind speed.

artery (ar′tər ē), the kind of blood vessel that carries blood away from the heart.

asteroid (as′tə roid′), a rocky object orbiting the sun between the planets.

atherosclerosis (ath´ər ō sklə rō´sis), a disease in which fatty substances build up on the inside walls of arteries.

atrium (ā´trē əm), one of two spaces in the top part of the heart that receive blood from veins.

axis (ak´sis), an imaginary line through a spinning object.

B

backbone, the main bone, made up of many small bones joined together, that runs along the middle of the back in some animals.

balance (bal´əns), an instrument used to measure an object's mass.

bar graph (graf), a graph that uses bars to show data.

barometer (bə rom´ə tər), a tool that measures air pressure.

behavior (bi hā´vyər), the way a living thing acts.

boiling (boi´ling) **point**, the temperature at which matter changes from a liquid to a gas.

bullhorn (bu̇l´hôrn´), an instrument with a built-in microphone that makes sound louder.

C

camouflage (kam´ə fläzh), any coloring, shape, or pattern that allows a living thing to blend into its surroundings.

capacity (kə pas´ə tē), the amount a container can hold.

capillary (kap´ə ler´ē), a tiny blood vessel with thin walls through which oxygen, nutrients, and wastes pass.

carbon dioxide (kär´bən dī ok´sīd), a gas found in air.

carnivore (kär´nə vôr), a consumer that eats other consumers.

cause (kȯz), a person, thing, or event that makes something happen.

centimeter (sen´tə mē´tər), a metric unit used to measure length; 1/100 of a meter.

chemical (kem´ə kəl) **change**, a change in matter that produces a different kind of matter.

chemical (kem´ə kəl) **energy**, energy that comes from chemical changes.

chlorophyll (klôr´ə fil), the green substance found in plants that traps energy from the sun and gives plants their green color.

classify (klas´ə fī), to sort into groups based on similarities and differences.

colony (kolʹə nē), a kind of animal group in which each member has a different job.

comet (komʹit), a frozen chunk of ice and dust that orbits the sun.

compass (kumʹpəs), a small magnet that can turn freely.

complex machine (komʹpleks mə shēnʹ), a machine made of many simple and compound machines.

compound machine (komʹpound mə shēnʹ), a machine made of two or more simple machines.

concave lens (kon kāvʹ lenz), a lens that is thinner in the middle than at the edges.

concussion (kən kushʹən), a condition caused by a sudden movement of the brain inside the skull, usually involving a brief loss of consciousness.

condense (kən densʹ), to change from a gas to a liquid state.

conductor (kən dukʹtər), a material through which electric current passes easily.

conifer (konʹə fər), a plant that makes seeds inside cones.

constellation (konʹstə lāʹshən), a group of stars that form a pattern.

consumer (kən süʹmər), a living thing that gets energy by eating plants and other animals.

context (konʹtekst), the parts directly before or after a word or sentence that influence its meaning.

continental (konʹtə nenʹtl) **shelf**, the shallow part of the ocean at the edge of the continents.

continental (konʹtə nenʹtl) **slope**, the edge of the continental shelf that extends steeply downward to the ocean floor.

control, the part of an experiment that does not have the variable being tested.

convex lens (kon veksʹ lenz), a lens that is thicker in the middle than at the edges.

coral reef (kôrʹəl rēf), a platform or ridge of coral at or near the ocean surface.

cubic meter (kyüʹbik mēʹtər), a unit for measuring the volume of a solid.

current (kėrʹənt), a riverlike flow of water in the ocean.

D

dark zone, the ocean water where sunlight does not reach.

decomposer (dē´kəm pō´zər), a consumer that puts materials from dead plants and animals back into the soil, air, and water.

density (den´sə tē), how much mass is in a certain volume of matter.

dicot (dī´kot) **seed**, a seed that has two seed leaves that contain stored food.

digestion (də jes´chən), the changing of food into forms that the body can use.

dormant (dôr´mənt), the resting stage of a seed.

dune (dün), a pile of sand formed by the wind.

E

earthquake (ėrth´kwāk´), the shaking of the ground caused by rock movement along a fault.

ecosystem (ē´kō sis´təm), all the living and nonliving things in an environment and how they interact.

effect (ə fekt´), whatever is produced by a cause; a result.

electric signal (i lek´trik sig´nəl), a form of energy.

electrical (i lek´trə kəl) **energy**, energy that comes from the flow of electricity.

electromagnet (i lek´trō mag´nit), a magnet made when an electric current flows through a wire.

ellipse (i lips´), the shape of a flattened circle.

embryo (em´brē ō), a tiny part of a seed that can grow into a new plant.

endangered (en dān´jərd), having a population that is falling low in number and that is in danger of becoming extinct.

energy (en´ər jē), the ability to do work.

enzyme (en´zīm), a chemical that helps your digestive system change food into nutrients.

erosion (i rō´shən), the moving of weathered rocks and soil by wind, water, or ice.

esophagus (i sof´ə gəs), the tube that carries food and liquids from the mouth to the stomach.

exoskeleton (ek´sō skel´ə tən), a hard outer covering that supports and protects some animals without backbones.

extinct (ek stingkt´), no longer existing.

F

fault (fȯlt), a crack in the earth's crust along which rocks move.

fertilization (fėr´tl ə zā´shən), the combination of sperm from a pollen grain with an egg to form a seed.

food chain, the flow of energy through a community.

food web, all the food chains in a community.

force (fôrs), a push or a pull on an object that can cause it to change motion.

forecast (fôr´kast´), a prediction of what the weather will be like.

fossil (fos´əl), any mark or remains of a plant or animal that lived a long time ago.

freezing (frē´zing) **point,** the temperature at which matter changes from a liquid to a solid.

friction (frik´shən), a force that slows the motion of moving objects.

front (frunt), the line where two air masses meet.

G

generator (jen´ə rā´tər), a machine that uses an energy source and a magnet to make electricity.

gills, organs for breathing found in fish and amphibians.

graduated cylinder (graj´ü ā´tid sil´ən dər), a tool used to measure the volume of liquids.

gram, the basic unit for measuring mass.

graphic source (graf´ik sôrs), a drawing, photograph, table, chart, or diagram that shows information visually.

gravity (grav´ə tē), a force that pulls any two objects toward one another, such as you toward the center of the earth.

H

habitat (hab´ə tat), a place where an animal or a plant lives.

hearing aid, an instrument used to help people with a hearing problem hear better.

herbivore (hėr´bə vôr), a consumer that eats plants.

hibernation (hī´bər nā´shən), a long, deep sleep in which an animal's heart rate and breathing are much slower than normal.

high blood pressure (presh´ər), a disease in which blood is pumped through the arteries with too much force.

high-pressure area (hī´presh´ər âr´ē ə), a place where cool air sinks and pushes down on the earth's surface with more pressure.

host (hōst), a plant or animal that is harmed by a parasite.

humidity (hyü mid´ə tē), the amount of water vapor in the air.

hygrometer (hī grom´ə tər), a tool that measures humidity.

I

indigestion (in´də jes´chən), one or more symptoms, such as stomachache, that occur when the body has difficulty digesting food.

inertia (in ėr´shə), the tendency of a moving object to stay in motion or a resting object to stay at rest.

instinct (in´stingkt), a behavior that an animal is born with and does not need to learn.

insulator (in´sə lā´tər), a material through which electric current does not pass easily.

K

kilogram (kil´ə gram), a metric unit of mass equal to 1,000 grams.

kinetic (ki net´ik) **energy**, energy of motion.

L

landform, a shape of the land, such as a mountain, plain, or plateau.

large intestine (in tes´tən), the last organ of the digestive system, which removes water and stores the waste material.

light zone, the sunlit waters of the ocean.

line graph (graf), a graph that connects point to show how data change over time.

liter (lē´tər), a unit for measuring volume.

low-pressure area (lō´presh´ər âr´ē ə), a place where warm air rises and pushes down on the earth's surface with less pressure.

M

magnet (mag´nit), anything that pulls iron, steel, and certain other metals to it.

magnetic (mag net´ik) **field**, the space around a magnet where magnetism acts.

magnetism (mag´nə tiz´əm), the force around a magnet.

mammal (mam´əl), an animal with a backbone that usually has hair on its body and feeds milk to its young.

mass (mas), the amount of material that an object has in it.

matter (mat´ər), anything that has mass and takes up space.

mechanical (mə kan´ə kəl) **energy**, the kind of energy an object has because it can move or because it is moving.

median (mē´dē ən), the middle number when the data are put in order.

melting (mel´ting) **point**, the temperature at which matter changes from a solid to a liquid.

meteor (mē´tē ər), a piece of rock or dust from space burning up in Earth's air.

meteorite (mē´tē ə rīt´), a rock from space that has passed through Earth's air and landed on the ground.

meteorologist (mē tē ə rol´ə jist), a person who studies weather.

meter (mē´tər), a unit for measuring length.

microphone (mī´krə fōn), an instrument used to amplify voices, music, and other sounds.

migration (mī grā´shən), the movement of an animal from one location to another as the seasons change.

milliliter (mil´ə lē´tər), a unit for measuring volume equal to 1/1000 of a liter.

mineral (min´ər əl), nonliving, solid matter from the earth.

mixture (miks´chər), two or more substances that are mixed together but can be easily separated.

mode (mōd), the number that occurs most often in the data.

molt (mōlt), to shed an animal's outer covering.

monocot (mon´ə kot) **seed**, a seed that has one seed leaf and stored food outside the seed leaf.

N

National Weather Service (nash´ə nəl weᴛʜ´ər sér´vis), a government agency that collects information about weather.

nerve cell (nėrv sel), a cell that gathers and carries information in the body.

nerve ending (nėrv en´ding), a tiny branch of a nerve cell that gathers information.

nutrient (nü´trē ənt), a substance in food that the body uses for energy, for growth and repair, or for working well.

O

ocean basin (bā´sn), the floor of the deep ocean.

omnivore (om´nə vôr´), a consumer that eats both plants and other consumers.

opaque (ō pāk´), does not allow light to pass through.

orbit (ôr´bit), the path of an object around another object.

ovary (ō´vər ē), the bottom part of the pistil in which seeds form.

ovule (ō´vyül), the inner part of an ovary that contains an egg.

P

parallel circuit (par´ə lel sèr´kit), a circuit that connects several objects in a way that the current for each object has its own path.

parasite (par´ə sīt), a plant or animal that feeds off another living thing and harms it.

photosynthesis (fō´tō sin´thə sis), a process by which plants change light energy from the sun and use it to make sugar.

physical (fiz´ə kəl) **change**, a change in matter that changes physical properties, but does not produce a different kind of matter.

pistil (pis´tl), part of a flower that makes the eggs that grow into seeds.

pitch (pich), the highness or lowness of a sound.

plasma (plaz´mə), the liquid part of blood that carries nutrients, wastes, and blood cells.

platelet (plāt´lit), a small part of a blood cell that helps blood clot and stops bleeding.

pole (pōl), a place on a magnet where magnetism is strongest.

pollen (pol´ən), tiny grains that make seeds when combined with a flower's egg.

pollination (pol´ə nā´shən), the movement of pollen from a stamen to a pistil.

pollution (pə lü´shən), anything harmful added to the air, land, or water.

potential (pə ten´shəl) **energy**, energy that an object has because of position.

precipitation (pri sip´ə tā´shən), moisture that falls from clouds to the ground.

predator (pred´ə tər), an animal that hunts and kills other animals for food.

predict (pri dikt´), to tell what will happen next based on what has already happened.

prey (prā), the animals that predators hunt.

producer (prə dü´sər), a living thing that uses sunlight to make sugar.

R

rain gauge (gāj), a tool that measures precipitation.

range (rānj), the difference between the highest and lowest number in the data.

recycle (rē sī´kəl), to use the same materials over and over again.

red blood cell, the kind of blood cell that carries oxygen to other body cells.

reflect (ri flekt´), to bounce back.

reflex (rē´fleks), a simple, automatic behavior.

reproduce (rē´prə düs´), to make more of the same kind.

reptile (rep´tīl), an animal with a backbone that has a dry, scaly skin.

resistance (ri zis´təns), a measure of how much a material opposes the flow of electric current and changes electric current into heat energy.

response (ri spons´), a behavior caused by a stimulus.

revolution (rev´ə lü´shən), the movement of an object around another object.

ridge (rij), the highest part of a chain of underwater mountains.

rotation (rō ta´shən), one full spin of an object around an axis.

S

saliva (sə lī´və), the liquid in the mouth that makes chewed food wet and begins digestion.

satellite (sat´l īt), an object that revolves around another object.

scavenger (skav´ən jər), an animal that eats dead animals.

sense organ (sens ôr´gən), a body part that has special nerve cells that gather information about the surroundings.

sepal (sē´pəl), one of the leaflike parts that protects a flower bud and that is usually green.

series circuit (sir´ēz sėr´kit), a circuit that connects several objects one after another so that the current flows in a single path.

simple machine (sim´pəl mə shēn´), a machine made of one or two parts.

small intestine (in tes´tən), the organ of the digestive system in which most digestion takes place.

solar system (sō´lər sis´ təm), the sun, the nine planets and their moons, and other objects that orbit the sun.

solution (sə lü´shən), a mixture in which one substance spreads evenly throughout another substance.

spinal cord (spī´nl kôrd), a thick bundle of nerves that connects the brain and nerves throughout the body.

spore (spôr), a tiny cell that can grow into a new plant.

stamen (stā´mən), part of a flower that makes pollen.

stethoscope (steth´ə skōp), an instrument used to hear the sounds of body organs.

stimulus (stim´yə ləs), the cause of a behavior.

symbiosis (sim´bē ō´sis), a special way in which two different kinds of living things live together.

T

tide, the rise and fall of the surface level of the ocean.

translucent (tran slü´snt), allows light to pass through but scatters it so that whatever is behind it cannot be clearly seen.

transmit (tran smit´), to allow to pass through.

transparent (tran spâr´ənt), allows light to pass through so that whatever is behind can be seen.

trench, a deep, narrow valley in the ocean floor.

V

vein (vān), the kind of blood vessel that carries blood back to the heart.

ventricle (ven´trə kəl), one of two spaces in the bottom part of the heart that pump blood out of the heart.

vibrate (vī´brāt), to move quickly back and forth.

visible spectrum (viz´ə bəl spek´trəm), light energy that can be seen and can be broken into the colors of the rainbow.

volcano (vol kā´nō), a mountain formed by hardened lava with an opening through which lava, ashes, rocks, and other materials come out.

volume (vol´yəm), the amount of space that matter takes up; the loudness or softness of a sound.

W

wave, the up-and-down movement of ocean water caused by the wind.

wavelength (wāv´lengkth´), the distance from a point on a wave to the same point on the next wave.

weathering (weTH´ər ing), the breaking and changing of rocks.

wind vane (vān), a tool that shows wind direction.

work (wėrk), the result of a force moving an object.

Index

Acknowledgments

Illustration

Borders Patti Green; **Icons** Precison Graphics

Front Matter J.B. Woolsey

Unit A 20, 27d, 74, 78, 108 Precision Graphics; 22, 27a-d J.B. Woolsey; 39c Ka Botzis; 70a Walter Stuart

Unit B 50 Walter Stuart; 78, 100, 101, 108, 109a, 112, 113, 117, 121 J.B. Woolsey

Unit C 9, 12, 13, 14, 27, 99, 100, 103b, 104 J.B. Woolsey; 40a, 53, 66, 67, 68, 79, 81 Precision Graphics

Unit D 11, 15, 23 Precision Graphics; 16, 21, 22, 24, 26 J.B. Woolsey; 42 Christine D. Young

Photography

Unless otherwise credited, all photographs are the property of Scott Foresman, a division of Pearson Education. Page abbreviations are as follows: (T) top, (C) center, (B) bottom, (L) left, (R) right, (INS) inset.

Cover: Lynette Cook/SPL/Photo Researchers; **iv** PhotoDisc, Inc.; **v** T Joe McDonald/DRK Photo; **v** B Michael Fogden/Animals Animals/Earth Scenes; **viii-ix** Background Leo L. Larson/Panoramic Images

Unit A
1 Spencer Jones/Bruce Coleman Inc.; 2 T Vincent O'Bryne/Panoramic Images; 2 CL Arie deZanger for Scott Foresman; 2 CR Arie deZanger for Scott Foresman; 2 Inset Nick Caloyianis; 3 C John Pade/Nelson/Pade Multimedia; 3 B Michael Stuwe; 8 David Young-Wolff/PhotoEdit; 9 William M. Smithey, Jr./Planet Earth Pictures (Seaphot Ltd.); 9 Inset John Neubauer/PhotoEdit; 10 B PhotoDisc, Inc.; 12 T Bill Beatty/Animals Animals/Earth Scenes; 13 T Runk/Schoenberger/Grant Heilman Photography; 13 T-Inset Runk/Schoenberger/Grant Heilman Photography; 14 TR Breck P. Kent/Animals Animals/Earth Scenes; 14 B Jim Corwin/Photo Researchers; 18 William J. Weber/Visuals Unlimited; 20 B Runk/Schoenberger/Grant Heilman Photography; 21 BL Mary Goljenboom/Ferret Research, Inc.; 21 BC Mary Goljenboom/Ferret Research, Inc.; 21 BR Mary Goljenboom/Ferret Research, Inc.; 38 Tom Bean/Tony Stone Images; 39 T Superstock, Inc.; 39 B R. Maler/IFA/Bruce Coleman Inc.; 40 T Zig Leszczynski/Animals Animals/Earth Scenes; 40 B Bob and Clara Calhoun/Bruce Coleman Inc.; 41 T Chris McLaughlin/Animals Animals/Earth Scenes; 41 C E. S. Ross; 41 B Chris McLaughlin/Animals Animals/Earth Scenes; 42 Bill Beatty/Visuals Unlimited; 42 Inset L. West/Photo Researchers; 43 T Jane Burton/Bruce Coleman Inc.; 43 C Frans Lanting/Minden Pictures; 43 B Tom McHugh, 1973, Steinhart Aquarium/Photo Researchers; 45 BR John Gerlach/Dembinsky Photo Assoc. Inc.; 45 TL James P. Rowan/DRK Photo; 45 CL Scott Camazine/Photo Researchers; 45 CR E. R. Degginger/Bruce Coleman Inc.; 45 BL Kramer/Stock Boston; 45 TR D. Lyons/Bruce Coleman Inc.; 46 PhotoDisc; 47 T Gary Meszaros/Dembinsky Photo Assoc. Inc.; 47 B Mark Moffett/Minden Pictures; 48 T Joe McDonald/DRK Photo; 48 B Wayne Lankinen/DRK Photo; 49 TR Mitsuaki Iwago/Animals Animals/Earth Scenes; 49 CR Wolfgang Bayer/Bruce Coleman Inc.; 49 CL Frans Lanting/Minden Pictures; 49 BR Marty Cordano/DRK Photo; 50 T PhotoDisc, Inc.; 50 B Art Wolfe/Tony Stone Images; 51 T Stephen Dalton/Animals Animals/Earth Scenes; 51 BL Dr. E. R. Degginger/Color-Pic, Inc.; 51 BR D. Cavagnaro/Visuals Unlimited; 52 Chuck Davis/Tony Stone Images; 53 T Renee Stockdale/Animals Animals/Earth Scenes; 53 C Julian Barker/National Gerbil Society; 53 B Julian Barker/National Gerbil Society; 54 Robert Maier/Animals Animals/Earth Scenes; 55 Leen Van Der Slik/Animals Animals/Earth Scenes; 56 T Steve Maslowski/Photo Researchers; 56 B Michio Hoshino/Minden Pictures; 57 T Leroy Simon/Visuals Unlimited; 58 Ralph Reinhold/Animals Animals/Earth Scenes; 59 Pat & Tom Leeson/DRK Photo; 63 Art Wolfe/Tony Stone Images; 68 L-Inset C. C. Lockwood/Animals Animals/Earth Scenes; 68 B PhotoDisc, Inc.; 68 R-Inset John Gerlach/DRK Photo; 75 Jose Carillo/PhotoEdit; 77 Lee Rentz/Bruce Coleman Inc.; 78 Patti Murray/Animals Animals/Earth Scenes; 78 T Kim Taylor/Bruce Coleman Inc.; 79 T M.H. Sharp/Photo Researchers; 79 BR PhotoDisc, Inc.; 79 BL Zig Leszczynski/Animals Animals/Earth Scenes; 79 CR Norman Owen Tomalin/Bruce Coleman Inc.; 80 CL Tim Laman/Wildlife Collection; 80 TL Joe McDonald/Visuals Unlimited; 82 R Rod Planck/TOM STACK & ASSOCIATES; 82 L Michael Gadomsky/Photo Researchers; 83 BL-inset Larry West/Photo Researchers; 83 R-Inset David Northcott/Superstock, Inc.; 83 Background Peter Cade/Tony Stone Images; 84 T Rod Planck/TOM STACK & ASSOCIATES; 84 CL Michael Gadomsky/Photo Researchers; 84 CR John Cancalosi/TOM STACK & ASSOCIATES; 84 B Tom Vezo/Wildlife Collection; 85 TL © Heather Angel ; 85 TC Larry West/Photo Researchers; 85 CL Lynn M. Stone; 85 TCR David Northcott/Superstock, Inc.; 85 CC Stephen J. Krasemann/DRK Photo; 85 CR Michael Durham/ENP Images; 85 BL Dwight R. Kuhn/DRK Photo; 85 BR Stephen J.

Krasemann/DRK Photo; 86 C Tony Freeman/PhotoEdit; 86 BL Michael Gadomsky/Photo Researchers; 86 BR Rod Planck/TOM STACK & ASSOCIATES; 87 L Larry West/Photo Researchers; 87 R David Northcott/Superstock, Inc.; 88 T David W. Harp Photographer; 88 BR Norman Tomalin/Bruce Coleman Inc.; 88 CL Frans Lanting/Minden Pictures; 89 T Patti Murray/Animals Animals/Earth Scenes; 89 CL Steve Winter/National Geographic; 89 CR Steve Winter/National Geographic; 93 Lee Rentz/Bruce Coleman Inc.; 98 R Peter Feibert/Liaison Agency; 98 L Bill Gallery/Stock Boston; 99 T Clifton Carr/Minden Pictures; 99 B Ken Cole/Animals Animals/Earth Scenes; 100 T HPH Photography/Wildlife Collection; 100 B Bruce Coleman Inc.; 101 T © Heather Angel ; 101 C John W. Matthews/DRK Photo; 101 B Michael Fogden/Animals Animals/Earth Scenes; 102 T Jim Brandenburg/Minden Pictures; 102 B Dr. Paul A. Zahl/Photo Researchers; 103 TR Frans Lanting/Minden Pictures; 103 CL Frans Lanting/Minden Pictures; 103 BR Jim Brandenburg/Minden Pictures; 104 B Fred Bavendam/Minden Pictures; 104 T Patti Murray/Animals Animals/Earth Scenes; 105 Scott Camazine/Photo Researchers; 106 B HPH Photography/Wildlife Collection; 106 T Erwin and Peggy Bauer/Bruce Coleman Inc.; 107 B ZEFA-Bauer/Stock Market; 107 T Mitsuaki Iwago/Minden Pictures; 108 L Francois Gohier/Photo Researchers; 108 C Patti Murray/Animals Animals/Earth Scenes; 108 R Dave B. Fleetham Marine Photographer/Visuals Unlimited; 109 T Jeff Foott/Bruce Coleman Inc.; 109 B Wayne Lankinen/Bruce Coleman Inc.; 110 TL Bradley Simmons/Bruce Coleman Inc.; 110 TR E.R. Degginer/Animals Animals/Earth Scenes; 110 BL F. Stuart Westmorland/Photo Researchers; 110 BR M.C. Chamberlain/DRK Photo; 111 T Art Wolfe Inc.; 111 B Zig Leszczynski/Animals Animals/Earth Scenes; 114 Owen Franken/Stock Boston; 115 T Townsend P. Dickinson/Image Works; 115 B Warren Williams/Planet Earth Pictures (Seaphot Ltd.); 116 Background Johnathan Nourok/PhotoEdit; 116 TR Michael Newman/PhotoEdit; 116 B Tony Freeman/PhotoEdit; 116 TL Richard Hutchings/Photo Researchers; 117 T Bob Daemmrich/Stock Boston; 117 B Greg Vaughn/TOM STACK & ASSOCIATES; 118 Mark J. Thomas/Dembinsky Photo Assoc. Inc.; 119 B John Obata/The National Tropical Botanical Garden, Lawai, Kauai, Hawaii; 119 C J. Beckett/American Museum of Natural History/Department of Library Services, Neg. No. 5367(4); 119 T Tom McHugh/Photo Researchers; 121 T Field Museum of Natural History, Chicago, IL/Neg.#GE086127C, photograph by John Weinstein; 121 B David M. Dennis/TOM STACK & ASSOCIATES; 123 HPH Photography/Wildlife Collection; 125 PhotoDisc, Inc.

Unit B
1 Tom Pantages; 2 T Vincent O'Bryne/Panoramic Images; 2 C Geoff Tompkinson/SPL/Photo Researchers; 3 B Alan L. Detrick/Photo Researchers; 3 C Dennis Potokar/Photo Researchers; 7 Kim Brownfield; 24 PhotoDisc, Inc.; 25 TL Binney & Smith; 25 TR Richard T. Nowitz/National Geographic; 25 CL Richard T. Nowitz/National Geographic; 25 CR Richard T. Nowitz/National Geographic; 29 NASA; 36 Al Bello/Tony Stone Images; 37 Milt & Joan Mann/Cameramann International, Ltd.; 38 Myrleen Ferguson/PhotoEdit; 42 Tony Freeman/PhotoEdit; 45 Jim Shippee/Unicorn Stock Photos; 48 Robert Clay/Visuals Unlimited; 77 Pekka Parviainen/SPL/Photo Researchers; 93 Michael Giannechini/Photo Researchers; 94 Michael Giannechini/Photo Researchers; 95 B Bruce Coleman Inc.; 95 C Robert E. Daemmrich/Tony Stone Images; 97 Background Lowell Georgia/Science Source/Photo Researchers; 97 TR-Inset Alfred Pasieka/Science Photo Library/Photo Researchers; 97 BR-inset Will and Deni McIntyre/Photo Researchers; 101 L Jeremy Horner/Tony Stone Images; 103 T Richard Megna/Fundamental Photographs; 103 C Richard Megna/Fundamental Photographs; 108 Mark Richards/PhotoEdit; 109 Myrleen Ferguson/PhotoEdit; 111 T Tony Stone Images; 112 T Harold Hoffman/Photo Researchers; 112 B Flip Nicklin/Minden Pictures; 118 Tom McCarthy/PhotoEdit; 119 BR Milt & Joan Mann/Cameramann International, Ltd.; 119 TR David Young-Wolff/Tony Stone Images; 120 T Hulton Deutsch Collection Ltd.; 120 B Hulton-Deutsch Collection/Corbis Media; 121 BR Jane Shemilt/Science Photo Library/Photo Researchers; 121 TL Jane Shemilt/Science Photo Library/Photo Researchers; 121 TR G. Thomas Bishop/Custom Medical Stock Photo

Unit C
1 Frank Siteman/PhotoEdit; 2 T Vincent O'Bryne/Panoramic Images; 2 CL NASA/Science Source/Photo Researchers; 3 B NASA; 3 C Hank Morgan/Rainbow; 8 PhotoDisc; 10 Greg Vaughn/Tony Stone Images; 15 T Felicia Martinez/PhotoEdit; 16 Barry L. Runk/Grant Heilman Photography; 17 Michael von Ruber/International Stock; 18 Craig Aurness/Corbis-Westlight; 19 T David R. Frazier/Photo Researchers; 19 BL John Lemker/Animals Animals/Earth Scenes; 20 T Mary Fulton/Tony Stone Images; 20 BL PhotoDisc, Inc.; 20 BR Johnny Johnson/DRK Photo; 27 Background Warren Faidley/International Stock; 28 L GOES Image/NOAA; 28 R GOES Image/NOAA; 29 Inset European Space Agency/Photo Researchers; 29 Ken Biggs/Tony Stone Images; 30 B Warren Faidley/International Stock; 30 T Charles Doswell III/Tony Stone Images; 31 Margaret Durrance/Photo Researchers; 37 Richard J. Green/Photo Researchers; 38 Leo L. Larson/Panoramic Images; 39 T Werner Forman/Corbis Media; 41 C Roger Werth/Woodfin Camp & Associates; 41 B Richard J. Green/